ALWAYS REMEMBER YOUR NAME

ALWAYS REMEMBER YOUR NAME

A TRUE STORY OF FAMILY AND SURVIVAL IN AUSCHWITZ

ANDRA & TATIANA BUCCI

Translated by Ann Goldstein

ASTRA HOUSE | NEW YORK

Originally published in the Italian language as *Noi, Bambine ad Auschwitz*,
by Andra and Tatiana Bucci. Collezione Strade blu, © 2018
Mondadori Libri S.p.A., Milan, Italy. First edition December 2018.

Photos courtesy of Andra and Tatiana Bucci.

For information about permission to reproduce selections from this book,
please contact permissions@astrahouse.com.

Astra House
A Division of Astra Publishing House
astrahouse.com
Printed in the United States of America

Publisher's Cataloging-in-Publication Data
Names: Bucci, Andra, author. | Bucci, Tatiana, author. | Goldstein,
Ann, translator.
Title: Always remember your name : a true story of family and survival in
Auschwitz / Andra and Tatiana Bucci; translated by Ann Goldstein.
Description: New York, NY: Astra House, 2022.
Identifiers: LCCN: 2021917176 | ISBN: 9781662600715 (hardcover) |
9781662600722 (ebook)
Subjects: LCSH Bucci, Andra. | Bucci, Tatiana. | Auschwitz
(Concentration camp) | Holocaust, Jewish (1939–1945)—Personal
narratives. | Holocaust survivors. | Jewish children in the Holocaust—
Biography. | BISAC BIOGRAPHY & AUTOBIOGRAPHY / Personal
Memoirs | BIOGRAPHY & AUTOBIOGRAPHY / Jewish
Classification: LCC D810.J4 B776 2022 | DDC 940.53/1503/92—dc23

First edition
10 9 8 7 6 5 4 3 2 1

Design by Richard Oriolo
The text is set in CenturySchoolbookStd.
The titles are set in Brixton_Wood-Vector.

We dedicate this book
to all the children of Auschwitz:
to the few who, like us, survived
and to the many who did not

My name is Liliana Bucci, but I'm called Tatiana.
I was born in Fiume on September 19, 1937, and I'm one
of the very few children who survived the
Auschwitz extermination camp.

I am Alessandra Bucci, but I've always been called Andra.
I was born in Fiume on July 1, 1939, and like my sister,
Tati, I'm one of the very few children who survived
the Auschwitz extermination camp.

CONTENTS

Translator's Note—by Ann Goldstein

ix

Foreword—by Ruth Franklin

xix

Map

xxvi

A STORY THAT COMES FROM FAR AWAY

1

THE NORMALITY OF HORROR

27

THE LONG ROAD OF RETURN

65

Afterword: A Journey into the Past Century
—by Umberto Gentiloni Silveri

151

Acknowledgments

163

About the Authors

165

About the Translator

167

Reading Group Guide

169

TRANSLATOR'S NOTE

IN JANUARY 2020, I received an email from Barbara Pierce, whom I didn't know, but who wanted to enlist my help in getting translated into English, and published, a book she had just read in Italian, *Noi, Bambine ad Auschwitz*, the story of two Italian sisters deported to Auschwitz at the ages of four and six. She had found the book deeply moving, and was passionate about getting it to a broader, English-speaking audience. She sent me the book, which I, too, found compelling and certainly deserving of a larger audience, and I agreed to start by translating a sample chapter. After trying various editors, publishers, and other avenues, we came to Alessandra Bastagli, the editorial director of Astra House, who is a translator of the survivors Primo Levi and Jurek Becker and publisher of other books about the Holocaust (including a book about Levi and a memoir by another Italian survivor, Piera Sonnino), and who was as enthusiastic as we were about publishing the book.

Three things struck me about *Noi, Bambine ad Auschwitz*: The first was that the sisters were so young when they were arrested and deported. The second was that the story's narrative voice is the first-person plural, the "we," and yet the authors beautifully sustain the sound of two voices, sometimes in unison and sometimes in dialogue; the insertions of one sister or the other into the "we" happen naturally and smoothly. Third, I was fascinated by the account of the sisters' lives after Auschwitz and of how they were able to return to the camp, both physically and emotionally, in order to tell their story to others, to bear witness. Not only that: I was also fascinated by how they came to the conviction that it was extremely important—crucial—for them to do this.

TATIANA AND ANDRA Bucci were born and spent their early lives in Fiume, on the Adriatic coast in what is now Croatia;

today it is the Croatian city of Rijeka. The family of their mother, Mira Perlow, were Russian Jews who, probably fleeing a pogrom, arrived in the port city, which was then part of the Austro-Hungarian Empire, in 1910. The family included Mira's parents, Rosa and Moise Perlow, and five of their six children (the sixth was born in Fiume), and Rosa's parents, Lazzaro and Lea Farberow, along with their six children and *their* children. From Fiume, many in this large family group continued on to America, but the Perlows remained (for one thing, apparently, they liked the fact that it was on the sea, so that it would be easier if they were forced to flee again). At the time of their arrival, nearly half the population of around fifty thousand was Italian, while the rest were mainly Croatian and Hungarian. There was a solid Jewish community, with many Jews having arrived in the 1870s and '80s, and a new synagogue had been built around the turn of the century. After the First World War, Italy and Yugoslavia both claimed Fiume, and it was briefly divided between them; in 1924 it was annexed to Fascist Italy and remained Italian until 1945. Moise Perlow seems to have gone off to fight in the First World War, from which he did not return. Tatiana and Andra's father, Giovanni Bucci, was an Italian Catholic, born in Fiume, who worked as a ship's cook and was rarely home. The sisters grew up with their mother's family.

In the fall of 1938 Mussolini announced the racial laws, which restricted the civil rights of Jews, excluding them from public schools, universities, politics, finance, the professions, and all sectors of public and private life. Thus, the children couldn't go to school and the adults lost their jobs; as the sisters write, "We spent some difficult months." Neither parent was religious, but with the promulgation of the racial laws Mira Perlow tried to catholicize her daughters by having them—and herself—baptized. In June 1940, Italy entered the war on Germany's side, which caused further hardships in daily life. Giovanni Bucci was on a ship off South Africa and was arrested and sent to a prison camp near Johannesburg, where he spent the entire war.

Although the racial laws were restrictive, people were able to live, as the sisters recall in an interview. Then, in July of 1943, Mussolini's government fell, and on September 8, Italy surrendered to the Allied forces. The Germans took over the country from Rome north. Fiume immediately became part of the Adriatic Littoral Zone under control of the Nazi-Fascists, and the deportation of its

Jews began. A poignant moment of the Bucci's story is the failure of their mother to find anyone who would be willing to hide them. Some members of the Perlow family fled, ending up in a small town near Vicenza, but they were eventually captured. In March of 1944 the Perlows remaining in Fiume were arrested; they had been informed on, they believe, by someone—an Italian—who worked in the synagogue (and who presumably received money for his information). Of the thirteen family members ultimately arrested and imprisoned, four returned.

TATIANA AND ANDRA arrived in Birkenau on April 4, 1944, and spent ten months there. For much of that time their mother was also there, and although her barrack was on the other side of the camp, she managed to visit them several times. In November she was transferred to another camp; she was then transferred to Buchenwald and eventually returned home after the war. The girls, however, remained in Birkenau, and were liberated on January 27, 1945, by the Russian Army.

We might expect that the sisters' story after the liberation would be a less absorbing one. But their path from the Polish city of Katowice to Prague, then to Lingfield, in England, and finally to Rome and then Trieste, where the family moved because Fiume had become part of Yugoslavia, is both dramatic and affecting. We should not forget that when they returned to their parents—an unusual and incredibly fortunate outcome—they were only nine and seven, and for almost two years had assumed their mother was dead.

When their family was reconstituted, there seems to have been a kind of unspoken agreement that no one would discuss the concentration camp experiences: the mother and daughters didn't talk, even to one another, about Auschwitz and its aftermath ("Between us," the sisters say of their mother, "was an impenetrable, total silence"), although the father spoke of his own five-year imprisonment in South Africa. The sisters talked about Lingfield House, a center outside London for children displaced or orphaned by the war, where they had a happy interlude and were able to regain something of their lost childhood. Their mother and aunt—the only other survivors in their family—told them how they had returned from the camps, but they didn't discuss it or ask the sisters questions. Their mother, as they say, seems to have made a determined effort to turn them toward the future, rather than the past, and enable them to construct "normal" lives for themselves.

In part, too, the atmosphere of the immediate postwar period was not conducive to the news from the camps: people did not believe what the survivors had to tell. Priorities were different: Italians were involved in rebuilding—themselves, their lives, their country—and wanted to cancel out the past. In an interview the sisters point out that when their mother returned, her friends asked where she had been, what had happened to her, but wouldn't believe what she told them: "'What are you talking about, Miretta?' they'd say." Primo Levi, in *If This Is a Man*, writes that it was the dream of every survivor—every prisoner—to tell, to relate, to recount; the nightmare was not to be believed. He called it "the story told and not listened to." Tatiana and Andra describe a moment during their adolescence when a sleeve slipped down as they grabbed the handhold on a bus, revealing the tattooed number: "People would ask if it was our telephone number, and we said yes. What should we have said?"

Eventually, however, they were able to talk about their experiences, and about how they reached that point. They began almost by chance, when, in the late seventies, they were interviewed for a book about Lingfield House. In the interview they said very little about Birkenau, since that was not the book's subject, but it was a first step toward confronting their memories. Also, the climate had begun to change, with organizations like CDEC (the Center for Contemporary Jewish Documentation) and, later, Steven Spielberg's Shoah Foundation actively searching for survivors who would tell their stories. Still, it was not until 1995—fifty years after their liberation—that the Bucci sisters began to speak more openly and freely about their arrest, deportation, and imprisonment, encouraged by other survivors and witnesses.

In 1996 the sisters returned to Auschwitz for the first time, an intense and difficult experience. Since then they have gone back numerous times, in particular with groups of schoolchildren, on so-called *Viaggi della Memoria*, or Memory Journeys. These are educational trips to twentieth-century historical sites related to the Holocaust, organized for students by Italian provinces, cities, or the Ministry of Education. Accompanying the students are historians and, in the case of the concentration camps, survivors and witnesses, who recount their stories and engage with the students. The students then write reports, make short films, and, most important, share the experience with their classmates.

TATIANA AND ANDRA Bucci are not professional writers; their account is unadorned, and perhaps for that very reason especially powerful. They did not allow themselves to be destroyed by the experience of Auschwitz. In part they attribute this to their mother's force of will, her strength of character, her determination to repress the past, and her insistence—both during imprisonment and after—on looking toward the future. They describe their lives as a mixture of the normal pleasures and troubles and struggles of existence: two ordinary women who have behind them an extraordinary experience of suffering and have managed to make something hopeful out of it.

—ANN GOLDSTEIN, NEW YORK, SPRING 2021

FOREWORD

BY ALL RIGHTS, this book should not exist.

The survival of anyone imprisoned in the vast death factory of Auschwitz is unusual enough. But the survival of a child is another matter entirely. Those tall or strong enough to pass—"eighteen," prisoners whisper to new arrivals in Imre Kertész's autobiographical novel *Fatelessness*, "tell them you're eighteen"—were treated as adults, laboring and suffering alongside the general population of prisoners. But almost all young children, as Tatiana and Andra Bucci acknowledge in their

astonishing memoir, were murdered by the Nazis immediately upon arrival.

Yet the Bucci sisters made it through not only the initial selection but three seasons at Auschwitz, surviving
until the camp was liberated by the Soviet Army on
January 27, 1945. The question of how they were able to
live is ultimately unanswerable, a reminder that despite
all the research conducted over the past seven decades
into the inner workings of the Final Solution, much of
what took place in the camps will always remain mysterious. There is a common perception that the Nazis ran
their extermination camps like a well-oiled machine, with
every cog lined up to generate murder with maximum
efficiency, but in fact much was up to chance. The mood of
a guard could spell the difference between life and death.

According to the official record, on April 4, 1944, 29
male prisoners and 53 female prisoners were selected
from the Bucci sisters' transport from Trieste and Istria;
the remaining 103 deportees, including Tatiana and
Andra's grandmother, Nonna Rosa, and their aunt Sonia,
were gassed. Perhaps, the sisters speculate, they were
spared because of their mixed parentage: their father,
an Italian sailor captured off South Africa when Italy

entered the war in 1940 and imprisoned near Johannesburg until 1945, was Catholic. Their mother had been
baptized together with the children several years earlier
as a precaution; after their initial arrest, she tried to
insist on the family's Catholic bona fides. Surely it was
her "quick-wittedness," they argue, that bought them life
in Auschwitz. But the likelier theory, which the sisters
also entertain, is that, at ages six and four, they looked
like twins—the special obsession of the infamous Nazi
doctor Josef Mengele. Disinfected and tattooed, they were
separated from their mother and taken to the *Kinderblock*, the barracks for children, most of whom were the
subjects of Mengele's notorious experiments.

The sisters write their memoir as adults; their book
benefits from the maturity of their perspective. But it is
always apparent that their memories of the camp are the
memories of children. (A note on terminology: the sisters
were held in the division of the camp known as Auschwitz
II/Birkenau, the extermination site and concentration
camp for Jewish prisoners, and usually refer to it as
Birkenau.) So young were they that Andra started wetting
the bed again—a problem for her sister, sleeping beneath
her. During the day they were allowed to play outside the

barrack, though of course there were no toys: "We play with nothing, only our imaginations." In the summer, they used pebbles, "because there's no grass around, just a lot of heavy gray mud." In winter, they tried to make snowballs, but, without gloves, their fingers were quickly frozen. No matter the season, their games were conducted amid "pyramids of corpses."

Most children at Auschwitz died within a year. The sisters survived, in part, owing to the attention of their mother, who managed to visit them occasionally, each time insisting that they repeat their names and their identity as Italians: perhaps because she wanted them to remember that they had a home beyond the camp, but also, more practically, so that she would be able to find them when they were inevitably separated. They also benefited from the goodwill of a *blockova,* or block leader, who brought them extra food and clothing and warned them not to volunteer when the guards offered a group of children a chance to "go see their mammas"—a cruel deception that brought about the death of their cousin Sergio. Andra remembers another "kind German" who gave them chocolate and white bread. More than anything, they had each other. "We stuck to each other like a stamp to a postcard," they write.

A pediatrician described the three hundred or so children discovered in Auschwitz at liberation as so starved that "the bones were the only part of their bodies that weighed anything." Because of their emaciated state, most were assumed to be younger than their actual ages. They had eye infections (possibly the result of experimentation), skin infections, bruises, even tuberculosis. The psychological damage, harder to quantify, must have been no less severe. At an orphanage outside Prague to which the sisters were initially sent, Andra locked herself in the bathroom rather than admit that she was sick, terrified of being taken to an infirmary like the one in the camp. Another child was punished for stealing soap—a justifiable theft after being forced to live in filth.

The turning point is the sisters' transfer to Lingfield House, a group home outside London run by Alice Goldberger, a German refugee who trained with Anna Freud. On a beautiful country estate, Goldberger—clearly a modern-day saint—managed to create a paradise of peace and security for survivor children. Surrounded by food, toys, and caring adults, the sisters were "reborn." One day, Goldberger showed them their parents' wedding photo and told them both of their parents were alive. Within months, the girls were repatriated to Italy. Reunited with their mother at the train station in Rome, they were thronged by people waving pictures at them, asking for information about their children's fate. In a later interview, Andra would remember how overwhelmed she felt by her inability to tell the crowd of bereft parents what they wanted to hear. "When these people asked me, 'Have you seen this person?' I would say, 'Perhaps I saw them.' Because I thought it was cruel to say, 'I didn't see them.'"

The sisters' mother "chose not to harass us with memories." She got rid of all artifacts from that period of their lives and refused to speak about the camp experience with them. "Between us was an impenetrable, total silence," they write. The contemporary reader might imagine such a silence as damaging. But the sisters prefer to see it as healing, "a way of protecting us." Not only did their mother not want them to suffer from what they would learn about her own experience, she wanted them "to look forward and not back." They returned to a life not unlike the one they had left behind, that of a "normal Italian family," and went on to marry and have families of their own. There are reminders throughout of those who were not as lucky, namely the sisters' aunt Gisella, Sergio's mother, who was never able to accept the truth about her son's fate, preferring to believe that he was still alive somewhere. "A child so lovely, she said to comfort herself, couldn't help being welcomed and cared for by someone in some corner of the world."

Over the course of this brief and spare book, I was surprised to find myself often moved to tears, particularly by the sisters' account of a teacher at Lingfield House who took Andra home with her and cuddled with her in front of a fireplace to help her feel safe. The International Tracing Service of the Red Cross had a "children's room" containing some three hundred thousand files: so many lost children, so many heartbroken parents. It is a consolation, however small, to know that a few of those children were, miraculously, welcomed and cared for by people whose kindness helped to make up for the brutality of others. The sisters reflect that it was not only the Germans who were responsible for the Holocaust but also the Italians and others who facilitated the Germans: "For this reason, too, we should all feel, in a small way, responsible for what happened." Yet many, too, worked to rebuild what the Nazis destroyed; and for them we can all feel thankful.

—RUTH FRANKLIN, NEW YORK, FALL 2021

Aucshwitz II Birkenau

Open-air cremation pits

Crematorium III

Crematorium II

Women's camp (starting July 1943)

Unloading ramp, arrival of transports, selections

Women's camp

Men's infirmary

Gypsy family camp

Men's camp

Women's transit camp

Family camp

Men's quarantine camp

Sector B I

Camp commandant's house

Kinderblock, barracks where Bucci sisters were housed

Sector B II

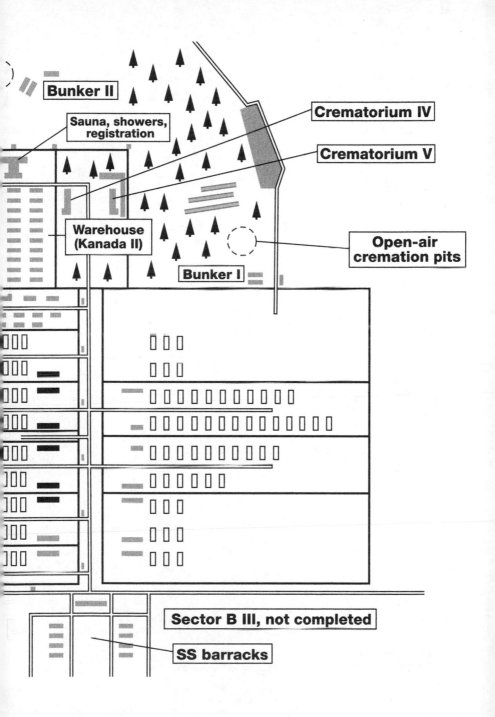

ALWAYS REMEMBER YOUR NAME

A STORY THAT COMES FROM FAR AWAY

FROM RUSSIA TO FIUME

Ours is a long story, and it begins far away. Our father, Giovanni Bucci, was born in Fiume into a Catholic family of Istrian origin. He met our mother, Mira Perlow, in Fiume in 1928; they fell in love and, seven years later, married. Mira, born in 1908 into a Jewish family, had arrived in Fiume as a child, with her parents, Moise and Rosa Perlow—our adored nonna Rosa, whom we grew up with until Auschwitz tore her from us. Nonna Rosa was born in 1883 into a family, the Farberows, who were then living in Vidrinka, a town on the border between Ukraine and Russia. According to her passport, which included her children, at the time of her birth and that of her children Vidrinka belonged to Russia. When she was a child, Russian (along with Yiddish, obviously) was the language spoken at home.

Around 1910—we don't know the exact year—Nonna, who had married Moise Perlow, left Vidrinka with her new family, almost certainly because of one of the many pogroms against the Jews that were raging throughout Eastern Europe at the time. Thus began a long period of wandering over the continent, a complicated journey that meant crossing borders and nations, passing through frontiers and peoples often hostile to the Jews. This was Europe in the early twentieth century, not long before the First World War broke out. The family traveled on horse-drawn carts, several generations together: our great-grandparents, Lazzaro and Lea Farberow, whose remains we found years ago in the Jewish cemetery in Fiume, and their children: Nonna Rosa with her husband, Moise Perlow; our great-aunt Rebecca with her husband, Salomon Plotkin; the Farberows' four other children; and a crowd of grandchildren and cousins.

This large group stopped for a short period in Hungary, where some relatives of Moise Perlow owned or managed a candy factory. But it was a brief stop; almost immediately the caravan decided to keep going, perhaps thinking that they might someday reach Palestine, perhaps simply looking for new opportunities. Eventually they reached Fiume, where they decided to stay, because it was a city on the sea, or so we were always told by our aunt Gisella, our mother's sister, who, although she was a child at the time, remembered those days. It was an interminable journey, she said.

So the Perlows arrived in Fiume from Russia before the Great War altered the map of the old continent, changing borders, affiliations, empires. Here, as often happened in those years, our family split up for the first time. The Plotkins continued on from Fiume to America, Uncle Salomon first, followed by his wife and children. They went to New York to seek their fortune, but after the war, with the death of Nonna Rosa and then of our aunts, we lost contact with our American relatives. (We found them again, somewhat by chance, several years ago, when Andra's daughter Sonia was trying, through the internet, to reconstruct our family tree. At that point

American descendants of the Plotkins got in touch with her, writing: "You know that we may be related?").

Of the six Farberow siblings who left Russia, only our grandparents decided to stay in Fiume: all the others went to America. Nonna Rosa decided instead to bring up her children in Fiume, with help from the city's Jewish community and with what she periodically received from the American relatives, and she had a respectable life, if without luxuries.

It's important to remember that until 1919 Fiume was part of the Austro-Hungarian Empire, and that, after a brief interregnum at the end of the First World War, it was Italian from 1924 to 1945. That's why we, who were born in the late thirties, felt and have always felt Italian. To a certain degree, our life is intertwined with the end of great European empires.

Nonna Rosa was very, very religious. She went to synagogue until the very last day—in January 1944, when the Nazis set fire to the building. But it wasn't a problem to be religious in Fiume. The Austro-Hungarian Empire certainly had many flaws, but it also had this distinctive characteristic: it didn't change your surname, it didn't oblige you to marry a faith, all were free to profess their own creed. Catholics, Jews, Muslims, Orthodox, and Protestants grew up together. The resentments and barriers or discrimination that always exist between people—because, unfortunately, they have always existed—were never sanctioned by the authorities. Rather, the contrary was true. It's a significant fact, and it allowed our grandmother to bring up her children in freedom. We think this was the reason that in the end the family chose Fiume as their home. One breathed a different air, the exact opposite of what the Farberows and Perlows had left behind: a long wake of fears, persecutions, and flights in search of peace and safety.

The Austro-Hungarian Empire was sustained by a particular environment, the Mitteleuropa of the early twentieth century, where our family, in spite of everything, including the many flaws and limitations of the system, could feel free. The culture in which Mira grew up was passed on to us as well: our mother instilled in us the principles of tolerance and respect, teaching us to see events and our own lives with an open-minded perspective. And she continued to encourage these principles even with what we suffered during the Nazi persecutions. It was an extremely important lesson, which helped form our characters and make us what we are today: Italian, but also citizens of the world.

In the house in Fiume, Nonna Rosa lived with her six children: Sonia, Gisella, Aaron, Mira (our mother), Paola, and Giuseppe (Uncle Jossi), born between 1902 (Aunt Sonia) and 1913 (Uncle Jossi, the only one born in Fiume). They all grew up like ordinary people, with ordinary aspirations, desires, uncertainties, and contradictions. Uncle Aaron, for instance, was very devout, unlike our mother, who was much less so and went to synagogue only on necessary holidays or when Nonna asked her to. The entire family, except our mother and Aunt Gisella, was murdered by the Nazis.

As we mentioned, our mother and father met in 1928. Giovanni (called Nino) was born in Fiume on June 24, 1906, and was therefore two years older than her. Papa was an extraordinary person. He was handsome and good: a very good man. His family had Istrian roots, and his surname was originally Bucich, Italianized after 1938 to Bucci, in another of those intersections and overlaps of history that have marked our family.

His mother, our paternal grandmother, was named Maria Salomon; she was Catholic, but she, too, probably had some remote Jewish roots. Nonna Maria ran a restaurant and partly for that reason our father learned to cook early. We never knew her husband, Nonno Tommaso; he was a sailor, who died on a ship transporting wood in the Strait of Messina when Nonna was pregnant with their third child. Papa had a brother who was an electrician and a sister, Aunt Antonietta (called Tonci), born around 1919, whom we were close to for a long time.

So Nonna Maria was Catholic and very observant, and maybe partly for that reason she wasn't terribly fond of us: she never accepted the marriage between Papa and Mamma, a Jewish woman joining the family. And she showed it on many occasions.

Our parents met under the clock tower in Fiume, the way young people did in those days, and as perhaps they still do today. They were engaged for seven years before they got married. Papa worked in a pastry shop and played soccer for the Fiumana team and for the national military team. He always said he should have gone to play for Bologna, which at the time was one of the most important teams in Italy. But life carried him elsewhere. He began going to sea, embarking as a cook. He loved ships. And he loved the sea, deeply. Even in the last years of his life, when he had retired, he would usually go out to the balcony as soon as he woke up to look at the sea. It was the first thing he did.

For many years he worked on ships belonging to Lloyds of Trieste, in the merchant marine. Most of his trips took him to the East: Africa and then, through the Suez Canal, as far as India. He had a profession and a passion that he pursued all his life. When he was traveling he constantly wrote letters, to Mamma and to us. It was a habit he had before the war and resumed afterward, when he started going to sea again.

We have no memories of him before the war, partly because we were very young, partly because he was always traveling, but mainly because he was imprisoned right away, in the first terrible months of the Second World War. In 1940, when Italy entered the conflict, he was sailing off South Africa. His ship, the *Timavo*, was sunk by its commander to keep it from being requisitioned by the British. Even though Papa wasn't a soldier, he was taken with the other Italians to Koffiefontein, a prison camp near Johannesburg. He stayed there until 1945. There, too, he worked in the kitchens. He found out about our deportation during his imprisonment. His family wrote to tell him what had happened to us. It's impossible to imagine what he must have thought or felt.

We were very young at the time; but our family was very close. During the years before we were deported, while Papa was a prisoner, Mamma made us kiss their wedding portrait every night, pointing to the figure of our father and repeating: "Send a thought to your adored papa." Precisely that gesture and that photograph allowed us to find the road home again, right after the horror of Auschwitz.

THE FAMILY AND THE RACIAL LAWS

We have some clear memories of our early childhood in Fiume, and some that are less distinct. Naturally Mamma and Aunt Gisella told us many things later. If we think back now, we return in memory immediately to our house, on the ground floor at Via Milano 15: we're inside, in a long hallway off which various rooms opened. We all lived there together: the two of us, Mamma, Papa when he wasn't at sea, Nonna Rosa, Uncle Jossi, and our cousin Mario, Aunt Sonia's son, who was about ten years older than us. He was born in 1928, and when our aunt moved to Trieste for work he stayed and lived with Nonna Rosa.

In Fiume our mother had become a seamstress, Aunt Gisella a milliner, and Uncle Jossi a barber. Mamma was very close to our aunt, who in 1937 married Eduardo De Simone; they, too, had met in Fiume. Following her husband, a sailor like Papa, to his various posts, Aunt Gisella moved to Naples, where, the same year, our cousin Sergio was born. Nonna Rosa attended synagogue regularly and was a dedicated member of the community, but that didn't make her narrow-minded or less open to the world: on the contrary. She was a very intelligent woman, and although she was devout, unlike our grandmother Maria she accepted the marriages of her daughters Mira and Gisella to Catholics.

We weren't wealthy, but we had a decent life. We were always well dressed, partly because Mamma was a seamstress, and it was important to her that we appear neat and proper when we went out. The handsome coats we're wearing in a photo with Sergio are her work. She was solidly integrated into the city, and had a lot of friends—especially outside the Jewish community—who remained close to her even after the promulgation of the racial laws, in 1938; it's not surprising that she married our father, an atheist from a Catholic family. They had a civil wedding.

In summer we went to the beach with our mother and grandmother; we always went to the same place, a pebble beach, not sand, right outside the city. Parties were organized for our birthdays: every year there was a photo with the date recorded on the back. Mamma really liked photography—she was crazy about it. The tradition of photographing our birthdays as if they were grand occasions was one that Tati continued for many years with her children. Formal portraits, if they can be called that, were, on the other hand, taken by a photographer, and for that Mamma always dressed us beautifully: it was an event.

As a good seamstress, she made over everything. She was extremely skillful. Even after the war, when whole boxes of fabrics and clothes arrived from our American relatives, Mamma was able to alter them according to what we needed. Once, finding some paper tissues in one of the boxes, we children said to each other: "Those Americans must be really poor if they can't even afford cloth handkerchiefs!"

We had, in other words, a normal life, at least until 1938, when things concerning our family began to change rapidly. First the racial laws, then the war and the deportations, transformed everything. Forever.

The first indication that something was changing was, in fact, the Italianization of our surname. Papa was summoned by his captain, who told him he had to change Bucich to Bucci, or he wouldn't be able to go to sea anymore. It was the first, immediate consequence of the politics of the Italianization of Istria imposed by the Fascist regime. In addition, he was asked to join the Fascist Party. That was the limit for him—a socialist forced to support the *fascio* (later he called himself a *nenniano*, a follower of the socialist politician Pietro Nenni). But like many others he couldn't refuse: he had a family to support. It was the sign of no return.

The second hint of the changing times was that Mamma was baptized, as an antidote to the imminent promulgation of the racial laws. Italy was suddenly becoming an unfriendly country. That was why Mamma decided to be baptized and to have us baptized, too, Tatiana in August 1938, and Andra when she was just born: an extreme attempt to safeguard us from the advance of history and the growing hostility toward the Jewish community in Italy.

With the laws of 1938 things also began to change in the family. All the uncles lost their jobs and Aunt Sonia was forced to return from Trieste. Our cousin Mario was obliged to leave public school and go to the school set up by the Jewish community in Fiume.

Tatiana, on the other hand, was still able to go to nursery school; we know this from pictures, because, naturally, we have very few memories of that period. The only memory Tati has is that one afternoon she cried and cried because Mamma had been a little late to pick her up.

The atmosphere at home quickly deteriorated, and we went through some difficult months. Mainly we were depressed: our family was being persecuted again. Worse, Mussolini had announced the racial laws in Trieste, practically in our backyard. It was like returning to a vortex that we couldn't escape. At the time, we didn't know that the future would be even sadder and more tragic, or that Mamma's attempt to protect us by having us baptized would turn out to be vain.

Meanwhile the war arrived. Like everyone else, we experienced the shortage of food and the other problems that the conflict brought to Europe: inflation, rationing, the black market. With Papa's salary, which fortunately continued to arrive even though he was a prisoner and far away, we were only just able to survive.

After September 8, 1943, things changed further, when the zone of Trieste and Fiume was incorporated into the area administered by the Reich. In the chaos and confusion of the autumn of 1943 Tati failed to enroll in first grade. We remember clearly running to the shelters in the winter of 1943–44, before our arrest; a soldier there had taken a liking to us and gave us candy.

Also, Uncle Eduardo, who had been recalled to fight by the Italian Navy, after September 8 was captured by the Germans and sent to a prison camp, where he remained until the end of the war. Thus Aunt Gisella, who that summer had come to Fiume with our cousin Sergio, decided not to return to Naples, since her husband wasn't there anyway. So we became a single nuclear family without the two sailors—our father and uncle—who were imprisoned far away. In hindsight, our aunt's decision to remain in Fiume was a terrible mistake, because soon after that the Allies liberated the south. After September 8, Italy was, in fact, cut in two like an apple: the center and the south finally liberated; from Cassino north occupied by the Nazi-Fascists.

Fiume, along with the provinces of Udine, Trieste, Gorizia, Pola, and Lubiana, became part of the Adriatisches Küstenland, the Operational Zone of the Adriatic Littoral, a territory under the direct administration of the Reich.

The occupation meant that Italian Jews would now be deported to the extermination camps scattered throughout the European countries that had come under the control of Germany and its allies. And so the trap opened that the Jews of Fiume, too would fall into. If Aunt Gisella had remained in Naples, maybe the story of our family, and in particular of Sergio, would have been different. But no one could ever blame her for it. None of us can know our own fate, especially in the midst of a world conflict. And there was nothing more natural for a woman left alone with a child in an unknown city than to go home to her own mother and her own family.

The summer of 1943 was very hot in Fiume, or at least that's how we remember it, maybe because, as a result of the war, we couldn't go to the beach for the first time. To cool us off a little, Nonna put the three of us—Sergio and us—in the bathtub, filling it with cold water. These are the first memories we have of Sergio. For us children, ignorant of what was happening around us and especially of the fate that would befall us, it was a lighthearted summer. It was the last summer we all spent together, while Europe burned.

In the winter of 1943–44, in fact, in a vain attempt to escape the Nazi threat, part of our family sought refuge far from Fiume. Uncle Aaron, his wife, Carola, and their son, Silvio, who was the same age as Tati, managed to hide for a while in Grisignano di Zocco, a small town near Vicenza. With them were Aunt Paola and Mario, Aunt Sonia's son, who was sixteen at the time. This is one of those small heroic stories of solidarity that should be known, the story of how a protective network was created in a small community that, for almost a year, managed to help and support a family of refugee Jews. Today in Grisignano di Zocco there is a small museum in memory of these events.

In November 1944, however, our relatives were all captured, turned in by some Italians. Uncle Aaron and the others were first transported by the Germans to Ravensbrück, since by late 1944 the transports to

Birkenau had been suspended. They died at different times and in different places: Aaron and our cousin Mario in Sachsenhausen, in April 1945; Carola, Silvio, and Paola in Bergen-Belsen, also a few weeks before the liberation. Our cousin Kitty Braun Falaschi, who was deported with them but survived, described little Silvio dying in his mother's arms during a transport and how she had sighed: "Finally."

ARREST

Mamma would have liked to find a place for us to hide, and she turned to Nonna Maria, who knew a lot of people in the small towns around Fiume. But no one helped us.

We don't know the exact day we were arrested. We know that we left for Auschwitz on March 29, 1944, because Mamma told us. So it was sometime in the last two weeks of March 1944 that the Nazis burst into our house.

The first memory we have of that night is the noise, the shouts and the uproar coming from the room next to the one where we sleep. Then Mamma enters our room, all out of breath, a clear image, carved into memory. She dresses us in a hurry: we have to get moving, we're leaving. We ask: where? why? But she doesn't have an answer to these questions.

We don't understand what's happening. Andra is still suffering the aftereffects of chickenpox and is slightly feverish. Memory goes to the table that is set for dinner. It seems likely, as we've reconstructed things over the years, that it wasn't very late when they came to get us. Mamma said it was around nine. We're a normal Italian family that, once the children are put to bed, prepares to have dinner. A dinner that is never eaten.

The second image, perhaps even stronger and clearer, is of our grandmother. Our beloved Nonna Rosa, dressed in black, as old, widowed women used to do, is on her knees, weeping and praying to a tall, impassive man, who is standing still and straight in front of her. She asks him to leave the children—take the adults but not the children. What fault do little children have? As if they, the adults, had ever had any fault. We feel no fear, but rather disbelief. We've never seen Nonna Rosa in such a state. We've never seen her cry. Tati remembers that she wasn't afraid but only pained at seeing her like that.

Years later we understood what then seemed incomprehensible and even mysterious. Nonna must already have understood, if not everything, certainly much of what would happen, maybe because of her memories as a refugee from the pogroms of Eastern Europe, maybe because of the rumors that were circulating about Jews being arrested, rumors that had driven part of our family into hiding. Or maybe because of something that had happened a few days before our arrest and that Mamma later told us: Nonna Rosa, looking out the window of our house, saw the person we think may have informed on us passing by. He wasn't a Jew, but worked at the synagogue and therefore knew many families who belonged to the community. He had reassured her: we were a family of modest circumstances, we had nothing to fear. Had it been a trap? A way to confuse her and prevent any idea of flight?

Mamma claimed that "our" spy, who had probably sold us out, was also present during the arrest. We never knew for certain. Maybe this *signore* rather than an informer was a "facilitator," someone who helped the Nazis, giving them information about the Jews. In any case, what we remember vividly is that the night of our arrest both

Nazis and Fascists entered our house. Germans and Italians. We were deported by the Nazis with the aid of Fascist Italians.

So we are dragged off, the two of us, Mamma, Nonna Rosa, Aunt Gisella, Sergio, Aunt Sonia, and Uncle Jossi. We leave the house abruptly, unable to bring anything with us, and are loaded forcibly into a car. We can't say what make or model, certainly it was big enough for all of us to sit in, us and our jailers. We remember shouts, orders, cries in Italian and German. We spend the night in Susak, Mamma tells us years later, a small village near Fiume. There was a building there where the SS held prisoners and interrogated them before sending them to the Rice Mill of San Sabba; the area was probably controlled by Franz Stangl, who had been the commander of the Sobibór extermination camp, in Poland.

The following day we go from there to our next destination. We cling to Mamma. Our gazes, our thoughts, are only for her. And so we have no memory of Sergio in these places. His image returns to mind only hours later, in the cell in the Rice Mill of San Sabba where all of us are locked up.

FROM THE RICE MILL TO AUSCHWITZ

From Susak they take us to the Rice Mill, the big rice-husking factory built in the late nineteenth century in the Trieste neighborhood of San Sabba, which, during the Nazi-Fascist occupation, changed aspect and function. After the armistice of September 8, 1943, and the creation of the Operational Zone of the Adriatic Littoral, it was used as a temporary prison camp for Italian soldiers. Then the Germans adapted it as a police detention camp. Here Italian, Croatian, and Slovenian partisans, political dissidents, draft dodgers, and civilian hostages were interned. For Jews it was, in the majority of cases, a place of transit before the final deportation. It also served as a warehouse for goods stolen from them.

Many people were killed, generally at night, and usually by hanging, though some were shot. The bodies of the victims were burned in a provisional crematorium oven, the only one in a camp on Italian soil.

We arrive at the Rice Mill in a truck, which drives directly into the large inner courtyard. We don't know how many there are in this first transport of ours, from Susak to San Sabba. Certainly the eight of us are all together. And we stay together in the cell that is assigned to us. It's a narrow cell, with a kind of bench. Our memory is of a cramped space; when we saw it again, years later, it seemed impossible that eight of us were locked in there.

We spend a few days at the Rice Mill; we don't remember exactly how many, partly because in prison all the days seem the same. Even as children we unfortunately understood that right away. We cling to Mamma the whole time. The adults take turns sitting on the bench, except for Nonna Rosa, obviously.

We almost never go out; we're given food through a small window. Only our mother (and maybe some of the other adults, we don't remember exactly) is taken away for several hours to be interrogated. She told us this years later, when she testified at the trial against the guards at the Rice Mill. The Germans probably want to know about other members of the family whom they haven't managed to capture yet. For a moment Mamma hopes that our being the daughters of a Catholic can in some way help us and allow her to save us. The woman who is interrogated before her, declaring that she is a Catholic, married to a Jew, asks that her children be freed. Exactly the opposite situation from ours. And when even that poor woman gets a curt denial from the guard, our mother maintains the illusion that she can save us. She isn't resigned to the evidence of an imminent tragedy. But it's a brief illusion. The Germans do not discriminate. To Mamma, who insistently points out Papa's religion, the soldier responds: "Doesn't matter. Jewish parent, Jewish children."

Our fate, our final destination, is the death camp of Auschwitz-Birkenau. The Germans have already decided this at the moment of our arrest in Fiume, considering all of us, equally, as Jews, including the two of us and Sergio, even though we're children of mixed marriages.

This is the first great turning point of our story: to be suddenly regarded as Jews and therefore sent to the Rice Mill, where the only way out was a convoy for Auschwitz. Much has been said on this subject, and we have talked about it at length with our friends and with the historians who over the years have helped us put our memories in order.

Our impression is that the Nazis, in Fiume and Trieste, made no distinctions. Get rid of them all, one less problem. Besides, the units that arrested us—and were in charge of the Rice Mill—were the same ones that years earlier had been part of Operation Reinhardt, on the eastern border of Poland: veterans of the killing operations in the extermination camps of Bełżec, Sobibór, and Treblinka, which had been active in Poland until a few months earlier. These units were famous for their cruelty and the speed with which they had been able to obliterate the presence of Judaism in Eastern Europe.

Of the two of us, it's Andra who has a clearer memory of our departure from the Rice Mill. Looking out from a balcony, she sees below, in the courtyard, a continuous coming and going of trucks and people. Today that balcony is no longer there; it collapsed. We, too, have to get into one of those trucks with the black tent over the back, to be taken to the square outside the Silos, a warehouse and freight terminal next to the main Trieste station, where our longer journey, to Auschwitz-Birkenau, will begin. The Germans loaded the prisoners onto the train for Poland from that square so as to avoid passing through the main station.

The image of the train car that we are forced to board is very clear. We are shoved into freight cars by uniformed guards, we don't remember of what nationality. There are very many of us. We're crowded into our car. We stay close to Mamma, standing, each of us clinging to one leg. The people are motionless. We're all silent, there's no confusion but, rather, fear, the anxiety to know where we're going. It's a silence that isn't a silence. Nonna is near us, with Aunt Gisella, Aunt Sonia, and Uncle Jossi.

In a corner there's a kind of bucket, maybe an oil can, for our needs, the women screening themselves with blankets, raised like a curtain by other women. Men and women, young and old, adults and children: maybe seventy people in all, but who can say precisely? Sergio is on the train, also clinging to his mother, Aunt Gisella. He has a frightened expression. And that remained with us, because we don't remember having, even here, a sense of fear or of terror. Tremendous disorientation, yes. Disbelief, stupor. Not fear. The train leaves. Now there's noise. A lot of noise: the clanging of the wheels on the rails, the people wailing, packed into that car heading toward the unknown.

Mamma manages to write a note with our names on it and throws it off the train, probably during a stop on the Brenner. Her hope is that someone will pick it up off the ground and send it. We know that Papa's family did receive it later. Maybe a railway worker found it and gave it to a carabiniere, who had it delivered to the addressees.

The sensations of the journey have never really left us. Often our minds return to those moments, but not, as one might think, when we're in a crowd or a chaotic situation. It's the sound of the train, its image, that strikes us. When Tati, for instance, sees a freight train go by, the sensations of those days resurface inside her.

It's an automatic reaction, which occurred for the first time quite a bit later, when we were adults, and were living in Trieste. During those years we lived near the port, and sometimes, coming home, you had to wait for the trains connecting the Central Station with Campo Marzio to pass. On a day like many others, the freight train that Tati sees going by in front of her—one like dozens of others she had seen passing on other occasions—recalls to her mind our journey to Birkenau. Since then it's been a recurring thought, an image that emerges from our memory in every station.

THE NORMALITY
OF HORROR

ARRIVAL AND SELECTION

Our arrival is mostly noise. It's April 4, 1944. The train stops outside the camp we're being taken to, which we later find out is Birkenau, the giant death factory in the concentration-camp system of Auschwitz. A place where hundreds of thousands of men and women are killed. People are calling out, looking for one another. Not all the families were able to travel together in the same train car, and as soon as they get off they start shouting the names of their loved ones. There are cries of fear as well, because dogs are barking and growling, because orders are given in German and almost no one understands them. There's tremendous confusion, in a ghostly scene of chaos.

Andra remembers the so-called *Judenrampe* outside the camp, where the deportees, having gotten off the train, are forced to line up for the selection. At that time, the trains didn't enter the camp directly, as they did later, when the Germans extended the tracks. The line is very long: first the women and children, then the men. Families are split up. And here they separate us from Nonna Rosa and Aunt Sonia, who are lined up where the trucks are and taken away. Forever. Whereas we remain in the other part of the line.

This is the second turning point in our lives. If the first, as we said, is connected to our final destination, Birkenau, now our fate is in the hands of a Nazi official who, with a nod, divides the people who will be interned from those, the majority, who are to be sent immediately to the gas chamber. Although children are generally killed right away, upon arrival, we escape the selection. It's a crucial moment, destined to mark our young lives.

Mamma keeps us close to her. We don't see our cousin Sergio. Maybe he has already been separated from our aunt Gisella, his mother, and put in the men's line, maybe not. We hold on to Mamma, and with her we walk down the long street that leads to the *Sauna*, the place where the few deportees who will enter the camp are tattooed and disinfected before being taken to the barracks.

Tati's memory of our arrival is, instead, fragmented: getting off the train and right afterward the *Sauna*. It's an endless trek, a tree-lined street, a very long way to walk in the dark, in the cold, with the fear of the unknown. Clinging to Mamma, we move slowly, surrounded by a crowd of people.

In the *Sauna* we have to give our personal information and then undress. We're naked, like the grown-ups. We are two little girls among women, who all look so pale to us and try to cover themselves with their hands. It's an incredible situation, fear mixed with astonishment and the embarrassment of seeing Mamma naked. She's always with us, she goes ahead of us at every stage, as if to protect us. This had never happened to us before. They make us walk in a line. In a small room the women's heads are shaved. Mamma loses her hair, but we're so terrified, frozen with fear, that we don't fully realize it. Our hair, instead, they leave. Right afterward they take us all to another room where they disinfect us: we're standing with our feet wet, as if we were in a pool; people are crying because the disinfectant burns in the cuts left by the shaving. It's a true inferno of noises, of smells; you breathe fear in the air. After we're disinfected they take us all into another big room for a shower: here, too, we're all together; here, too, the shame and embarrassment of being naked.

Then we're given clothes that are not ours; they're too big and very light. They'll never protect us from the cold.

This is the moment when we're tattooed. We're pushed into a vast room; at the far end of this crowded space there's a small table, as small as a school desk of long ago. A man and a woman are sitting there. They have a kind of pen nib, like an old-fashioned pen, which they dip in the ink. Mamma is ahead of us, with her head shaved: she's the first of us three to be tattooed, she wants instinctively to protect us again, to find out if it will hurt. Her number is 76482. Then it's our turn. They begin to tattoo us. So many tiny dots. First Andra, her number is 76483; then Tati, her number is 76484. In our memory as children we don't feel any pain. Small pricks of a needle stuck in our arm, imprinting a number that will be with us our whole life.

Andra learned her number by heart almost immediately, Tati didn't—and when she had to repeat it she always had to read her arm. Only when, in recent years, we began to tell our story did she manage to learn it by heart. It has always been part of her, she says it's as if she'd been born with it.

Also in the *Sauna* is Aunt Gisella. She, too, is tattooed: 76516. But Sergio isn't there. He must have been in line with the men, after us. Maybe with Uncle Jossi, who was registered with the number 179603 and died in October 1944. Sergio's number is 179614. He was put in the camp, too, it's not clear why, spared immediate death in the gas chamber.

We are often asked why we were interned and not killed immediately with our grandmother and aunt Sonia. Basically death was the fate of almost all the children who arrived at Birkenau. Only a tiny, almost insignificant percentage entered the camp. Even smaller is the number of those who survived. We don't have an unambiguous answer. Some say it's because they thought we were twins, which is plausible, since if you look at pictures of us at the time we really do look alike. (In fact we were assigned to the barrack that housed the children, including twins, whom the Nazis used for their experiments.) But we have no evidence, only hypotheses.

More likely, we and Sergio escaped immediate death in the gas chamber because, as children of mixed marriages, we were not considered "pure" Jews. Almost certainly, we think, it must have been due to our mother's quick-wittedness; during the selection on the ramp she must have insistently emphasized the Catholic branch of our family, declaring, as she had at the Rice Mill, that we were the daughters of a Catholic. There, on the ramp, our fate was sealed. There where, with a look and a simple gesture, the Nazis shifted you from the line of those who were to be sent immediately to the gas chamber to the line made up of the very few who were to be interned (and in the end, obviously, killed as well, like the others). Mamma, who during our imprisonment never lost heart, certainly must have said something to protect us right at that moment. She must have understood that in a few seconds someone would decide whether we would stay alive or be eliminated.

LIFE IN THE CAMP

When the tattooing is over and we come out of the *Sauna*, we are separated from Mamma. We're wearing clothes that don't belong to us, and shoes that are too big. We walk with a woman, perhaps German, who wears what seems to us a military uniform, a skirt and jacket different from what the prisoners have. Now, again, we have to walk a very long way. Our barrack is near the entrance to the camp, on the exact opposite side from the *Sauna*.

We enter and our immediate impression is that it's huge. It's rectangular in shape, like the ones that can still be seen today at Birkenau. Our memories of the barrack's structure don't always coincide. A *blockova*, the barrack guard, is waiting for us, and we're handed over to her. She's probably Polish; later we learned that in general the *blockovas* were ordinary prisoners assigned to that job. She leads us to our beds, which are near the entrance. One for each of us, in what looks like a long row of bunk beds. Our memory of those moments is made up of images and emotions. We don't know what we said to each other the first night. We don't remember sleep or hunger or thirst. The actual photograph that we still have today is of the two of us clutching each other, as if to protect each other. We don't see Sergio. He doesn't enter the barrack with us. At some point he, too, arrives, but we couldn't say how much later.

Ours was a *Kinderblock*. It wasn't the only one in the camp; we learned later that there were other barracks for children. But we didn't see them; we stayed in our world, Barrack No. 1, where there were children from various places, most of them destined to be victims of experiments.

In our bunks there are no sheets, only an extremely thin mattress and a harsh, rough blanket, like a military blanket, which doesn't protect us from the terrible cold we feel. In the middle of the barrack is a wood stove with a big pipe, but its effects are nonexistent. With those temperatures, it would have to stay lighted continuously to warm the space. Although Andra is the younger, she's given the top bunk; Tati gets the one below. Here Andra starts having problems with bed-wetting. After all, it was an extremely difficult situation, almost intolerable: our first night in the barrack, the first time in our life without Mamma. Andra's bed-wetting isn't a problem only for her but also for Tatiana, who is sleeping underneath her.

So the next day we change places and Tati climbs up to the top level of the bunk bed. Andra has the same problem almost every night, starting the first one we spent in the barrack, our new home. She stopped bed-wetting only when, after the liberation, we arrived in England.

The *blockova* has her own bed near the entrance, on the right, in a sort of recess. She doesn't pay much attention to what we do, only the bare minimum. We quickly understand that, from her point of view, we're going to die. In the months of our stay in Birkenau we also discover where she keeps the secret box in which she hides the objects she finds wandering through the camp or steals from the prisoners. She takes it out in front of us, thinking she has nothing to fear from two little girls, and when she opens it necklaces and other pieces of jewelry appear. Maybe valuables that came from *Kanada*, the place where some of the internees are forced to collect, inspect, and sort the baggage of the new arrivals—both those destined for the gas chamber and the very few entering the camp—who are thus robbed and stripped of everything.

Our memory of the ten months we spent in the camp is of an apparent normality. Of course, it was a normality that was constructed only in our minds. Two little girls, alone in an unknown place, with adults we'd never seen before. Fear must have been inevitable. But in our memory it was replaced by that sense of normality that children often create to defend themselves in the face of the most terrible events, the unexpected. Andra attributes that sensation to Tatiana's protectiveness toward her. Tatiana was the older one, so maybe Mamma had told her to take care of her younger sister, or maybe it was instinctive. Probably both. The fact is that the entire time we stuck to each other like a stamp to a postcard.

But fear erupts aggressively when, every so often, an adult wearing a white coat enters the barrack to take away some of us children. At the time we knew nothing about the medical experiments. All we saw was that some children went away and didn't come back. Those who were taken didn't return. That was very clear to us. And our fear became terror.

Our life in the camp was punctuated by an alternation of fear and terror. And yet even in these situations children manage to find the resources to construct an intelligible universe around themselves. It's what happened to us, when, to combat the fear, we immersed ourselves in the absurd daily life of Birkenau, trying by that means to survive.

Summer and winter are superimposed in our memories. Some episodes are vivid, carved into our minds; others are faded. At night we sleep with our clothes on. We don't remember washing or how we took care of our physiological needs, but surely, like everyone else, we used the toilet, if you can call it that, available to the prisoners: a hole inside the barrack with a wooden lid.

Cold is a constant sensation, and the thin jackets we wear don't protect us. Food and hunger are vague memories. We're given a watery broth to eat, a sort of tasteless minestrone. Each of us has a bowl and a spoon, which we keep hidden under our pillows or in the pocket of our clothes. And then there's the smell, a constant smell of burning, probably from the chimneys that are almost always in operation. At first we don't realize what's happening to us. Only after a while do we understand that we have to stay there because we're Jewish. We figure it out from what the *blockovas* say, from the way they talk about us.

In the barrack, boys and girls are separate. The number of children changes, according to the "needs" of our jailers, that is, by how many are taken to become guinea pigs in experiments, how many are killed or transferred. All of us wear dark, very thin clothing. We don't have a clear memory of the other child prisoners. Their presence and our games are vivid in our minds, just like any episodes, any images. But there are no faces, we can't remember or visualize a single face, a single expression. Apart from Sergio, of course, and a very few others, but only because we met them again afterward.

Among the ones we remember is Julius Hamburger, a Slovak who, before coming to Birkenau, had already been in various other camps. Today he lives in Israel. He was a couple of years older than Tatiana. He brought us food, and helped us in whatever ways he could, us and the other smaller children. He must have been a truly clever and generous kid. And then there were the Traubova sisters, Hanka and Eva. They were younger than Andra. We were together with these three children during the liberation, when, after the Russians arrived, we were taken to the orphanage in Prague. We remember them as our companions in the barrack because we somehow reconstructed that fact afterward. In the testimony that Julius gave after the liberation, he spoke about the two of us, citing us by name.

During the day, we're allowed to play outside, but always near our *Kinderblock*. We play with the other children, girls with girls, boys with boys. For that reason, too, Sergio isn't always with us. He's more often with the boys. In the morning we children feel that in a certain sense we're "masters" of the camp: it appears to be mostly empty, since the majority of the adults are forced to work. We play with nothing, only our imaginations, because we certainly don't have dolls or toys, or other games. We have pebbles in summer, because there's no grass around, just a lot of heavy gray mud. In winter we throw snowballs, but we don't have gloves. And if you make snowballs without gloves, you can't make more than one or two, because your fingers freeze.

Death is everywhere around us. And yet, strangely, we're not afraid of it, and we quickly get used to this parallel reality. We are always seeing the corpses of adults. Bodies piled in a corner, heaped up in a barrack, transported by other prisoners. But to us it seems ordinary. We play around what Tati calls the "pyramids of corpses": white, skeletal, striking. We both have a vivid memory of them. In the morning, a rectangular wooden cart, with sides, goes from barrack to barrack collecting the dead. A terrible job, if we think back on it now, carried out by two prisoners: one takes the corpse by the arms and the other by the legs, they swing it and then give a sharp heave to hoist it to the top of the pile of bodies. Once, the cart arrived with a dead man covered by a white sheet. Andra asked: "Why the white sheet?" Someone answered: "Because he's a German."

Today these images seem intolerable to us, but at the time they didn't upset us. At a certain point Andra thinks that all this is nothing but the "normal" fate for Jews. Nothing other than the life we have to have. And even Tati convinces herself that this is simply her natural place: being Jewish means living and dying like that in Birkenau. A thought that works its way into our childish minds without other explanations or clarifications.

Wandering around the camp, past the piles of corpses, we see, from a distance, the chimneys of the crematoriums that continuously spit flames and smoke. Always, night and day. We can also see them from outside our barrack. The smoke shifts with the wind. We know that's where "you go out." And even the idea of "going out through the chimney" seems normal to us. It doesn't surprise us. After a while we understand the use of the chimney. Someone must have explained it. Or maybe we heard it from the *blockovas*, or from some older child.

Normally we have no contact with the adults. We don't talk to anyone. Only with the other children and, minimally, with our *blockova*, mainly when we're carrying out her orders. Once, Tati encounters a young man who is probably a guard, though he seems almost a boy. He's walking on a street in the camp near our barrack, which the adults call Lagerstrasse. He's wearing a uniform, or so it seems to her. He comes up to her with a box of cookies in his hand. A square tin box. Tatiana remembers only the box, not eating the cookies. Probably we shared them with Sergio, and maybe with the other children. Today, we can't explain that man's gesture, who he was or why he came to us. The Germans almost never entered the camp. They observed and directed things from the outside. Contact with the prisoners was kept to a minimum.

Near our barrack are barracks that house only women. In one of them the *blockova* loves to punish the prisoners. We can't say how many times we saw an orderly row of women, on their knees on the gravel in a kind of courtyard, forced to hold two bricks in their raised hands. It's a terrible scene. The *blockova* inflicts this torture on the prisoners repeatedly. Few of them wear the striped uniform: they're dressed in normal clothes that by now are reduced to rags, with old shoes or even barefoot. But we know they're prisoners. We can wander among them, but we're forbidden to talk to them or go near them.

This *blockova,* who is so cruel, behaves with odd compassion toward us. The *blockovas* wear dark clothes, not the striped outfits. And they wear skirts. The one in the women's barrack is also a little overweight, and her jacket doesn't fasten properly. Maybe it's because they have regular meals. Every so often she brings us something different to eat. She's taken a liking to us. We don't know the reason, but it's precisely her care for us that later saved our lives. She also gave us two white angora sweaters. We remember it distinctly because we had never had sweaters like that in Fiume. One day she calls us over and gives them to us. We aren't surprised: we're struck more by the sweaters than by the gesture itself. We don't feel it as a special favor.

By that time we spoke German, the language of the camp, which we, like all the other children, had to learn quickly. That was the language used among us small prisoners: gestures at first, then German (also because there weren't any other Italian children).

Andra remembers being in the hospital. It must have been for just a few days, otherwise, as often happened to those who were sent to the hospital, she wouldn't have come out alive. Maybe because of the aftereffects of chicken pox, which she still had the day of our arrest. Her memory is sometimes clear, other times confused: she's sick and spends her days on a bunk bed. The hospital, basically, is similar to the barrack we live in. They put her on an upper bunk. She spends a lot of time lying on her stomach. On one of those days an incident takes place that's forever stamped in her memory. There's confusion. And noise, a lot of noise, so much that she covers her ears with her hands. A woman is lying on a cot, a few meters away. A man in a white coat goes by, places his hand on Andra's head as if to push it down, under the pillow. He tells her not to look. Isn't that the best way to stimulate a child's innate curiosity? And as soon as he goes away, Andra starts peering through the crack between the boards at the edge of the bunk. The woman lying there is weeping: she's giving birth. There's a lot of blood. Andra is really upset. After a while she understands that a child is being born, or rather has been born. We don't know what happened to the woman or the child.

Mamma also came to see Andra in the hospital. It's an extraordinary fact, because the infirmary of Birkenau was as different as possible from a normal hospital, with visits and all the rest. But Mamma was like that. As long as she, too, was a prisoner in Auschwitz she never lost sight of us. Even today we don't know how she did it, and yet she managed to find her child in the hospital. She must have bribed the *blockovas*, maybe giving up her bread ration, or maybe offering some objects that Aunt Gisella, forced to work in *Kanada*, managed to steal. These are only hypotheses. Certainly she had an insane courage, and ran tremendous risks. It wasn't easy to move safely and for no reason through the camp; in fact it really was impossible.

Our situation as little girls left partly free to roam around—as we waited for our fate to be decided by the prison guards or by the criminal doctors who used the children in the barrack as guinea pigs for their inhuman experiments—was completely anomalous for Birkenau. After all, Birkenau was an extermination camp, in which the few interned prisoners—that small percentage of people who, getting off the trains or trucks, were not sent immediately to the gas chamber—were called by the Nazis "corpses on vacation." They were only manpower, "pieces," as the Nazis said, or slaves to be used until they wore out before being murdered. Unlike us children, the detainees had no freedom of action, they could move around the camp only on precise orders. The punishments for those who disobeyed were harsh, death the norm. But the strength of our mother's love for us was greater than the fear of being punished or killed. Mamma was always like that. From the day of our arrest, she never relaxed her vigilance, which had a single objective: to save us children. She was determined to live and have us live. After the war she told us how in prison she would always wash her underpants and attach them to her back to let them dry, because otherwise someone would steal them. She wanted to wash, even in those harsh conditions, at whatever cost. She wanted to remain human. That was her will, her determination.

And that's why she also managed to come and see us in the children's barrack. We don't know how long after our internment she started coming, nor could we say exactly how many times she came in the period between April and the end of November, when she was transferred. Maybe five times? Maybe more? She would arrive near evening, after the long workday, exhausted. We would meet her for a very short time outside the barrack. We could still recognize her, although she no longer had hair, and was extremely thin and emaciated. In our memory there is also fear: we had trouble accepting her, she was so changed. Fear drove us, in a way, to reject her, made it difficult to let go and hug her, as when children want to make adults feel guilty. Certainly she must have suffered from it, but she must also have understood that ours wasn't an ordinary situation. She was too intelligent, our mamma.

Those evening encounters are a precious memory. Thinking back on them today, we feel a sea of emotions tossing inside. She would arrive, hug us, kiss us, and the first thing she did was repeat our names to us. She said: "Remember, your name is Liliana Bucci." "Remember, your name is Andra Bucci." She did it with a precise purpose, which we understood only later. We didn't have a roll call like the adults, we didn't have to learn our number by heart the way they did. Our names were everything. Mamma wanted to keep us attached to our real life, the one outside the camp. Or maybe she was already thinking of the day of our liberation, of two little girls alone in the middle of Poland. There's no way of knowing. After the war, we never spoke to Mamma about these episodes. Between us was an impenetrable, total silence.

Sergio doesn't appear in these memories, either. There's only Mamma and us. It's possible that he was with Aunt Gisella, who might have come with Mamma to see us. But we can't say with certainty. These are only fleeting impressions. Despite the absurdity of the situation, the suggestions that Mamma gave us had results, so that Tati forgot the family nickname she'd always had and still does, and became Liliana, the name that appeared on documents and that Mamma repeated to her at every encounter.

One evening, Andra recalls, Mamma informed us that she wouldn't be coming anymore. The vision of death was such an unvarying element of our world that in the following days, when she didn't show up, we were both convinced that she had died. And it seemed to us completely normal, it didn't surprise us. We took it for granted that the adults in Auschwitz died: we saw so many of the dead around us.

THE STORY OF SERGIO

We have a very clear memory of the day Sergio left Birkenau for Hamburg. It's what most tortures us, an obsession of our life after the war. One day, the *blockova* of the women's barrack, the one who seemed more kindly toward the two of us, told us that the next day all of us children would be assembled and would be asked if we wanted to see our mammas. The Germans would take ten boys and ten girls. We must not put ourselves forward, she told us, for any reason; we must refuse the offer. She didn't add any explanation. We assured her that we would obey, maybe partly because Mamma herself had told us that she wouldn't come to see us anymore, and we already believed that she was dead. Obviously we reported to Sergio what the *blockova* had told us. We told him what would happen and that he shouldn't volunteer, either, for any reason.

The next day, in fact, they assembled us all outside the barrack. It was the end of November, and almost our cousin's birthday. A man arrived; this time he wore a normal uniform rather than a white coat. We don't know who he was. Maybe a camp official or maybe Dr. Kurt Heissmeyer himself, a Nazi doctor known for performing experiments on human guinea pigs. He asked us the question we expected: "Who wants to go and see Mamma?" We remained motionless as statues. But Sergio came forward. Tati remembers that he took a step out of the line, Andra that he raised his hand. Maybe both, it's not important. What matters is that our warnings had been in vain. His desire to see his mamma was too strong. How could you blame him, after all. With that cruel trap the Nazis demonstrated not only their brutality but also their treachery and cunning. For Sergio the call of his mother was irresistible. There were two of us, and we had been used to sticking together ever since we were small. Not Sergio: at the time he was an only child. Not until after the war did our aunt and uncle have another child, our cousin Mario. Sergio's mother was truly everything to him; probably he suffered from her absence more than we did from the absence of our mother.

The SS collected the twenty children who had been so insidiously chosen and led them to the ramp: they were happy, they didn't cry and didn't complain, because they thought they were going to see their mothers. We waved to them with hands raised, we saw them leave. That we remember clearly: all twenty getting into a train car, looking at us from behind a barrier. It was an atrocious trick. Twenty little children carried off under the illusion that they would see their mothers. Inside we knew that we wouldn't see them again. Obviously we weren't certain: it was a sensation, maybe due to the strong bond we had with Sergio, or to the environment we were in, where, if a person was taken away, he or she didn't come back. We also remember that from then on our barrack was definitely emptier, because almost no children arrived, as no more transports arrived at Auschwitz. It was the last time we saw Sergio.

It took us a long time to be able to talk about what happened to him, except, naturally, when we returned to Italy, and our aunt and uncle questioned us closely.

But there are other stories within this tragic episode. Lives brutally cut off as the war was ending and the Nazis had lost. For example, in our barrack there were two brothers: one, like Sergio, chose to go; the other remained. The latter, a survivor like us, we saw again in

Israel long afterward. Every year he goes to Hamburg to honor his brother. There was a boy who had just arrived in the camp and chose to go with the group of twenty, sharing their fate. His parents, too, like our cousin's, had another son after the war, whom we met in Hamburg and who wanted to know what we remembered of his brother.

The story of these unfortunate children, including Sergio, was reconstructed some time after the end of the war. For many years Aunt Gisella and Uncle Eduardo's attempts to discover what happened to him had no result. Of course, their hopes remained alive, especially after we returned home. They wrote to all the humanitarian organizations that were involved in helping refugees and war orphans in those years. A few years ago we received a folder from the International Tracing Service (ITS), in Bad Arolsen, regarding Sergio. The ITS is the center for research on deportees that was set up by the International Red Cross at the end of the war. Requests arrived from all over Europe, mainly from people asking for information about their family members. The officials opened a file for every request received and put all pertinent information in it: correspondence with the families and with other organizations that were helping refugees scattered throughout Europe, the searches that had been undertaken, the results. At the headquarters of the ITS is a so-called "children's room," which contains three hundred thousand files, among them Sergio's. As the documentation makes clear, there was no shortage of clues over the years that our cousin might have been found, but unfortunately it always turned out that there had been a mistake or it was the wrong person.

Not until the early eighties did we learn his fate, thanks to Günther Schwarberg, a German we came to respect and admire, and his wife, Barbara Hüsing. These two journalists stumbled on the tragic story of the twenty children murdered after serving as human guinea pigs for the atrocious pseudoscientific experiments of Dr. Kurt Heissmeyer, the Nazi medical officer who tortured Sergio and the others. Piece by piece, with great patience and perseverance, they managed to put together the whole story.

After the war, Heissmeyer had gone back to practicing as a doctor. Eventually, he was arrested and, in 1966, went on trial. He was given a life sentence and died a year later in prison. At the trial, the truth about the fate of the twenty children in Hamburg came out. During the arguments, perhaps thinking that he would give scientific validity to his brutal activities, Heissmeyer himself quoted the clinical records of the children who were brought from Birkenau to Hamburg in late November 1944 and tortured. Twenty innocent children who, after the experience of Auschwitz, were forced to undergo, first, injections of tuberculosis bacilli and then the removal of lymph nodes from their armpits. (There are even photographs, taken by the Nazis to document the experiment, in which Sergio and his companions, heads shaved and bare-chested, have their right arms raised to show the incision in their armpits.) At the end of the experiment all twenty of these little guinea pigs were murdered, by hanging, during the night of April 20, 1945, in the basement of the Bullenhuser Damm school, in Hamburg.

The story of Sergio and the nineteen other victims was told in Schwarberg's *The Murders at Bullenhuser Damm: The SS Doctor and the Children* (1979; published in English in 1984). The story has not been forgotten, because Günther and Barbara, along with other friends and colleagues, created a foundation, the Vereinigung Kinder vom Bullenhuser Damm (Children's Association of Bullenhuser Damm), dedicated to preserving the memory of that tragedy and to making it known.

The work of reconstruction done by Schwarberg and Hüsing is a story within the story, in which the will to see justice done clashed with the omissions and repressions of some in Germany in the postwar era.

Schwarberg died in 2008. Today in the school in Hamburg where the children were massacred there is a memorial honoring Sergio and his companions. In the mid-nineties, in the same neighborhood, twenty streets were renamed for the victims. In the beautiful cemetery in Hamburg, in the section dedicated to Italian victims of the Second World War, there is a stone to Sergio's memory, placed in 1995.

Uncle Eduardo died in 1978, before he could know the truth of his son's fate. This was in part because Sergio's name wasn't reported clearly in the documentation, and it took Schwarberg and Hüsing a long time to identify him. Aunt Gisella, on the other hand, who survived Auschwitz and died in 1988, learned the truth but never accepted it. She was asked to come to Hamburg, to testify at the trial of some of the criminals who had participated in the murder of her child. Mira Tatiana, Andra's daughter, who spoke German, accompanied her on that journey, which took place in 1983 or 1984. But our aunt was unable to testify. She refused, because she could in no way accept the truth about her son. She couldn't accept it. And who would have been able to, after all? She always told herself, with conviction, that Sergio was still alive: a child so lovely, she said to comfort herself, couldn't help being welcomed and cared for by someone in some corner of the world.

OUR LIBERATION

Then comes the day of our liberation. It's January 27, 1945. Here, too, our memory fades. Andra has a clear image of Russian trucks moving along the main street of the camp, of vehicles going back and forth. We understand that something unusual is happening because the soldiers wear uniforms we don't recognize. And because they're smiling. Yes, smiling. Then a type of jeep stops in front of us. A soldier is sitting on the hood. He wears a beret with a red star. Andra remembers him vividly. He has a small wooden board on his knees, on which he's cutting a piece of salami. He looks at us, offers it to us.

A spontaneous, natural gesture, unthinkable in Birkenau. It's the two of us, our small prison companions, and this Russian soldier who offers us some salami. That, for us, is the liberation.

A few days later, we were taken to Katowice, about fifty kilometers from Auschwitz, where, in the children's ward of the hospital, the Russians had assembled all the children they'd picked up during their march as they liberated this part of Poland. Not only Jews, of course: the orphans and refugees were from all cultures and all nationalities.

We are often asked what happened to our fellow prisoners from Birkenau, and whether they came with us to Katowice and then to Prague. All we know for certain is that the confusion in those weeks was overwhelming, and many organizations, from the Red Cross to the Jewish groups, were trying to help the refugees by reuniting families and fates. By some chance in life, we were sent from Katowice to Prague.

Fiume, December 5, 1935. Mamma and Papa on their wedding day. This is the photo we kissed every night before going to bed while Papa was imprisoned in South Africa.

Fiume, early thirties. Almost the entire Perlow family. Standing, from left: Aunt Paola, Aunt Gisella, and Mira, our mother. In front: Uncle Aaron, Nonna Rosa, and Uncle Jossi.

Fiume, summer 1943. We three cousins—Sergio, Tatiana, and Andra— and behind us, standing, our mother, Aunt Paola, Nonna Rosa, and Aunt Gisella, who was spending the vacation with us.

Fiume. Tatiana (third from left) in a picture taken at nursery school.

Fiume. The house on Via Milano where, until our arrest, we all lived together: the two of us with our parents, Nonna Rosa, Uncle Jossi, and Mario, Aunt Sonia's son.

1943. Mamma liked taking pictures of us, but formal portraits, like this one of Tatiana, were taken by a photographer.

Aunt Gisella and Sergio lived in Naples, but they spent long periods in Fiume, because Eduardo De Simone, Sergio's father, was a sailor and often far from home.

Mamma was a seamstress and made marvelous dresses, like the one worn by Andra on her fourth birthday.

Sergio was arrested with us and interned in Birkenau in the same *Kinderblock*.

From left: Aunt Paola, Aunt Gisella, and Mamma; in front, we three cousins in summer outfits.

Summer 1943. Sitting on the sidewalk with Sergio, we're taking a break from our games.

Mamma was very protective of us, but also strict.

From left: Mamma with her sisters and we three cousins, during a summer spent together in Fiume.

November 29, 1943. Very stylish in our winter coats, made by Mamma, we're celebrating Sergio's birthday with him.

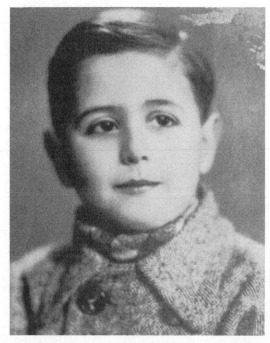

Fiume, 1943. Sergio was used by the Nazis as a guinea pig and then hanged at the Bullenhuser Damm school, in Hamburg.

Uncle Aaron, Nonna Rosa, and Mario, the sixteen-year-old son of Aunt Sonia, who lived with us in the house on Via Milano.

Mario as a child. After hiding with other family members near Vicenza, he was arrested and killed at Sachsenhausen in April, 1945, at the age of sixteen.

Silvio, the son of Uncle Aaron, was deported to Bergen-Belsen and died in the arms of his mother, Carola, during a transport.

Prague, 1946. At school for the first time, Andra learned to write, but in Czech.

Tatiana, who couldn't bear the orphanage, erased even the memory of the room where she slept with her sister.

Lingfield, 1946. In Surrey, Andra finally started to smile again and play like a child of her age.

Trieste, summer 1947. Reunited with Mamma and Papa, we are again a happy family, but at home we avoided talking about what had happened to us.

Auschwitz-Birkenau: students listening to Andra and Tatiana during the Lazio Region Memory Journey. With them are Nicola Zingaretti, at the time governor of the province of Rome, and Piero Terracina and Sami Modiano, also survivors and witnesses.

Birkenau. Andra between Walter Veltroni, the mayor of Rome, and the Shoah historian Marcello Pezzetti during a Memory Journey with students from Rome. In 2004 the City of Rome decided to make these journeys a regular event.

THE LONG ROAD OF RETURN

PRAGUE

The image immediately following that of the camp's liberation is the train journey to Prague, the Czech capital, where we arrive in the spring of 1945. Andra even remembers the station underpass, lined with white tiles. In Prague we were taken to an orphanage, a place we were never able to find again, even when, many years after the war, Tati returned with her husband to look: no one knew anything about it. The orphanage was an enormous building that housed a large number of children. When we arrived no one asked us about the camp, about our family, about our past, maybe because there were so many children like us that our condition was considered "normal." Tati remembers one girl who was extremely thin, with a big, swollen belly: the typical empty stomach that we can still see today in disturbing images from Africa. Who knows what that poor girl had suffered.

In Prague, we also went to school for the first time. Because of the racial laws, Tati hadn't been able to go to school in Italy. Every morning, we were taken from the orphanage to this huge building with a massive staircase at the entrance. The school was run by nuns, and there both of us finally learned to write, even though it was in Czech.

We remember the first day of school very clearly. And the atmosphere, the air you breathed: gray, with nothing cheerful or carefree about it, the way it should have been. The sisters also used a rod in class. It wasn't cruelty; it was an element of the harsh methods of a time when adults were generally very rigid, rarely loving and warm toward children. All of us had—some in one way, some in another—survived the war or the camps. And yet nothing was forgiven. Once a child was forced to go up the stairs with a sign attached to his back that said: "I must not steal soap." That was emblematic.

In Prague, Tatiana began to have intense, and unexpected, migraine attacks. She would spend the morning with her head in her arms, resting on the desk, trying to make the migraine go away. The migraines didn't diminish until, a year later, we arrived in England, but even today from time to time she suffers from them. Also in Prague, Andra was taken to the hospital: she had locked herself in the toilet for hours and wouldn't come out. She was ill, very, but was afraid to say so. She was afraid she would be taken to an infirmary where she might relive the chilling moments in the infirmary in Birkenau.

Life in Prague was so grim that we've erased from our memory even the room we slept in. We don't remember it. And yet we were there for more than a year, from the spring of 1945 to April of 1946. We learned Czech and forgot Italian completely, recovering it only some years later, when we returned to our family. With others we spoke this new strange language, Czech, while with each other, instead, we continued to use German: it was our "secret language," in which we thought we could communicate without being understood by strangers. We were certainly better-off here than in Birkenau, because we were fed and weren't cold. But in Prague, too, the absence of affection or sympathy on the part of the adults was total. Nothing. For the same reason, we didn't make friends with anyone, with the children or with the teachers.

In Prague, we knew only two things: that we were Italian and that we were Jewish. It was a reality that we had learned very well in the camp. And so when, one day, all the children were asked: "Who of you are Jewish?" we stepped forward. Julius Hamburger and the sisters Hanka and Eva Traubova, who, as we said, had been with us in Birkenau, also came forward. And it was our salvation. What a paradox! Being Jewish, which had caused us to suffer the most atrocious, inhuman, and unjustified wrongs at the hands of the Nazis, now saved us, taking us away from a place that we really didn't like, thanks to an English Jewish humanitarian organization that facilitated the return home of orphans who had survived the persecutions. We found out later that, in the preceding months, other Jewish children had left Prague.

The five of us, then, boarded a small military plane. It was our first airplane trip, but we don't remember it with any special emotion: it was only another of the many relocations we had endured. We got in and sat in the military seats, keeping our seat belts fastened during the whole flight to avoid the jolts from air pockets. The plane didn't have windows, so we couldn't see out. We looked at each other. Here was another unexpected journey toward an unknown fate, even if this time the adults who were our escorts looked after us and helped us. Our destination, we soon found out, was Lingfield House, near London, in great and victorious England.

LINGFIELD HOUSE

At Lingfield we began to live again. There we finally recovered our childhood, which had been lost and stolen. It's a wonderful and indelible memory, one of those memories that stay with you and make you nostalgic but are also very comforting.

We landed in England on an April evening in 1946. The five of us got in a car to drive to a small town in Surrey. We had no idea where we were going. Surely we must have been told, but in our memory we didn't know what was happening. We drove down a long tree-lined avenue, at the end of which was a beautiful building. It was a typical English country house, with a garden around it and vine-covered walls. Here was the true feeling of the countryside of southern England.

As we later found out, the house belonged to Sir Benjamin Drage, an English Jew who had kept a small wing of the building for himself and his family, and given the rest to the English Jewish community to be used as a home for deported children from all over Europe.

The story of Lingfield has been told in a wonderful book, *Love Despite Hate* (1983), by Sarah Moskovitz, which talks about us and reports our testimony. And it demonstrates that, in the face of the tragedy that struck millions of people, including hundreds of thousands of children, there were also experiences of profound fellowship. Many international organizations, not only Jewish, were engaged in helping the war refugees and survivors of the Nazi deportations. In early 1945 in England, the Committee for the Care of Children from Concentration Camps launched an appeal to take in orphans from Europe. The idea was to organize a number of residences that would welcome the children, giving them a home and restoring their sense of self. Sir Benjamin made his small estate at Weir Courtney available; that was where we were being taken.

Alice Goldberger, who had arrived in England in 1939 from Berlin, where she had run a center for disadvantaged young people, was chosen to manage Lingfield House. Although she had declared herself an anti-Nazi, at the outbreak of the war Alice, as a German citizen, was confined on the Isle of Man. There she started a school for the children of the families of internees that was much written about in the English newspapers. She was released in 1942 under pressure from Anna Freud, who wanted Alice to work with her in London.

The daughter of Sigmund and Martha Freud, Anna, born in Vienna and then, with her parents, forced to find refuge abroad, specialized in child psychology and was already an authoritative figure in the British cultural panorama. At the start of the war, she created the Hampstead War Nurseries, an institution that assisted children who were victims or refugees of war. It was Anna Freud and Alice Goldberger who were the true guiding spirits of Lingfield House, an extraordinary institution that, between 1945 and 1957, took in more than seven hundred children, helping them recover their sense of self and self-esteem. Goldberger was supported by the psychologist Oscar Friedmann and some thirty colleagues and nurses who took care of the children. Among them was another remarkable woman whom we had the good fortune to meet and who cared for us in the months we spent in England: Martha (Manna) Weindling Friedmann.

The center had begun its work some months before we arrived (the first group of children had come from Prague in August 1945). As soon as we got there we were taken to a room full of toys. It was a real Land of Toys for us, who hadn't touched a toy in more than two years. And what toys! There was an enormous dollhouse, with rooms and furniture and all the rest; an almost life-size horse; and a lot of little cars. It may seem silly, but when we entered that room of toys we felt instantly revived. It was an almost immediate sensation—our hearts skipped a beat. And this was only one of the many rooms in the house. It was very big, and was divided into two parts, with an iron gate that separated the two different halves. Behind the house was a paddock where there were horses. The kitchen had a glass door looking out onto the garden, which had a small swimming pool.

We shared our bedroom with other girls. It was lovely, with wallpapered walls. Our beds were soft and clean. There were night tables and a window that looked onto the green and flowering garden; ivy climbed up the window frames; and next to the beds were chairs, where—as they taught us to do—we put our clothes, neatly folded, when we went to sleep at night. It was a habit we kept in the years following our return to Italy. Placed on the blankets was a soft inflated thing we'd never seen before: a hot-water bottle to warm the bed. Things that ordinary people considered normal were for us an extraordinary discovery: so extraordinary were the hot water bottles that we asked to have them taken away, since we were used to sleeping at very different temperatures.

At Lingfield we immediately felt loved. The women who took care of us had a very clear idea of what we needed: affection and empathy. Right away we felt welcomed and protected—yes, protected. So much so that Tati, for the first time, felt freed from having to keep track of her sister at every moment. That mixture of affection and sense of duty that had been with her for two long years finally gave way to the carefree mood of childhood: to the right to be a child.

Tati made friends with a girl from Czechoslovakia named Miriam Stern. Her mother had entrusted her, with her sister Judith, to a peasant family in an attempt to save them from deportation. Judith was found and sent to Ravensbrück; Miriam remained hidden in an attic for two years. Incredibly, when the war was over the two sisters managed to be reunited and now were at Lingfield House. Tati spent a lot of time with Miriam, which caused Andra to suffer—she felt abandoned. But these were normal reactions: on the one hand the wish to be carefree, on the other the younger sister's sense of abandonment. Andra was jealous, even if she didn't say so and tried not to let it show. Photographs from the months we spent in the cottage portray us together at meals, obviously, and in games in the garden; but there were also many moments when we were apart. Not until years later did Andra have the courage to admit the weight of her jealousy.

In the first days the assistants tried to get us to talk, and asked us to tell our stories. We repeated our names— as Mamma had taught us to do in Birkenau—and we explained that we were Italian. We spoke in German, because we hadn't yet learned English. And, besides, the women who ran the cottage were almost all German refugees who had come to England with the advent of Nazism, in the early thirties. We told them what we remembered of our lives, and that our parents were dead. After all, we had heard nothing of our father, while for us our mother had died in Birkenau. Then they told us that we shouldn't speak German anymore. Probably with the change of language Anna Freud also wanted to help us emerge from the nightmare we had been plunged into. We continued to speak Czech with each other; for a while, with other people, we spoke German and then, after we had full-immersion learning, English.

It was important for us to speak English because it was the language used by the other children. We have wonderful, vivid memories of our companions at Lingfield. Altogether there must have been between twenty and thirty children. Not all came from the camps, like us; many had been hidden in cities or in the countryside. There was Zdenka, an orphan from the ghetto of Theresienstadt, and one of the first to arrive at Lingfield; a pair of Hungarian siblings; and Fritz, who had been afflicted with polio, and his sister Hedi and their aunt Magda. There was Ruth, who came from Czechoslovakia and stayed to live in London, becoming English; there was Miriam and her sister Judith, who remained the longest at Lingfield House. It's Judith who, several years after the center closed, donated many documents and photographs regarding the center and the children who stayed there to the Holocaust Memorial Museum in Washington, where they are archived.

Our days passed in a round of school, meals, and moments of play and fun. Alice Goldberger was the coordinator; and a group of girls (the two of us, plus Miriam, Zdenka, and Hanka) were assigned to Manna Friedmann. She became a sort of adoptive mother, or, rather, a new aunt. She had left Germany when she was twenty to join a brother who was studying at the university, and had had no more news of her Orthodox Jewish family. Anna Freud was very much present. Andra spent a lot of time with her, and she let Andra use the loom where she wove in her free moments.

When we were truly settled, we were also given special jobs. We "older" children (Tati was nine, Andra seven) were charged with taking care of the younger ones. In particular at night, at bedtime, we had to help them take a bath and put on their pajamas. Andra had a difficult, lively girl to look after.

Thus at Lingfield, in spite of everything, we began to have a normal life again. We celebrated birthdays, we had games in the garden, and every weekend we put on a little play on a small stage set up in front of the pool. We'd mount the stage and perform. Andra remembers playing the part of the Princess and the Pea; Tati, once, the prince or something like that.

There were also fire drills once a month. We hated them!

One day, the Queen Mother came through the town of Lingfield. We were lined up on the sidewalk, among the residents, flags in hand, and we sang. She was wearing a light-colored dress and she waved at us from the car.

Occasionally we'd go on a bus trip with the other children. We went to the beach and often to the zoo. We also went to the movies in London: we saw Walt Disney's *Pinocchio*. We ate a lot and well, all together at the same time. There was milk, meat, cereal, cornflakes, fruit: so much abundance compared to what we had, later, in Italy. In Trieste, right after the war, very few people even knew what bananas were, let alone cornflakes. At Lingfield we were taught to sit properly at the table, to peel fruit and eat it with a fork and knife, to knit, to wash, and to fold our clothes carefully before going to bed. When we returned to Trieste we insisted on explaining to Mamma how to do it!

We were also taught Hebrew, in case we should ever go to Israel. Sir Benjamin, the owner of the estate, came by now and then to see us. He was tall and large, and very kind: he often gave us apples.

At school they put us in separate classes. Tati adjusted easily; she made friends with a classmate, and even visited her at home. There's a photo of them together, in which the English friend is holding a kitten. Andra, on the other hand, had more problems adjusting. In the entrance hall there were lockers; the children were supposed to leave their things there and then go to the classroom. Instead, Andra, when she arrived, stopped and sat on a bench in the hall, waiting for the teacher to come and get her. The teacher became interested in her case. She asked Alice Goldberger for permission to take her home for a weekend. She had a nice two-story house where she lived with her husband. They welcomed Andra like a daughter, gave her a bath, drying her and cuddling her as they sat in front of the fire. They helped her overcome her fear of strangers. From then on Andra went to class without any trouble, like everyone else. She needed to feel warmth around her. Her difficulties, her fears, are recounted in the letters we eventually sent from Lingfield when our parents managed to track us down in England.

Some years ago we returned to see our English home. After having been abandoned, it was bought by a wealthy man who, when he found out the "secret" that the building guarded, decided to restore it to the way it was then, in homage to its remarkable history.

We also saw some of our friends from that time, whom we'd lost contact with when we returned to Italy to be reunited with our parents. We'd lost contact partly because the institution was moved to London, partly because it was the wish of our teachers: to burn the bridges to the past in order to encourage a return to normal life. The meeting happened, as such things often do, a bit by chance, in 1978; Mamma was living in Trieste then and one night she got a call from a correspondent for an English TV show, *This Is Your Life*. It was on every week and each program was devoted to a particular person. The correspondent was calling because the producers were preparing an episode on Alice Goldberger and were looking for children from Lingfield House to interview as witnesses of that experience.

They knew only that our name was Bucci and that we lived in Trieste. They found Mamma by the simplest method: calling all the (few) Buccis in the phone book. Mamma gave them our addresses (at the time Andra was living in Padua and Tati in Brussels). They got in touch with us and asked us to come to London, to take part in the broadcast. (It aired on the BBC on October 25, 1978.) Mamma came with us, too.

Thus we saw many of our friends from Lingfield House, including Miriam, who had gone to live in California. We recognized one another right away—instantly. It was truly an emotional moment. It seemed as if we'd parted the day before and yet almost thirty years had passed. And Alice Goldberger was also overcome by emotion when, suddenly, she saw us appear: her children of Lingfield House.

HOME AT LAST

One day, our time at Lingfield ended. We don't know exactly when: it must have been September or October of 1946. Alice Goldberger called us to her office. That struck us immediately, because, although she was the director, she didn't have daily contact with the children. So to be summoned by her meant that something important had come up. She showed us some photographs, one in particular. It was our parents' wedding photo that we had kissed every night before going to bed in Fiume, when our father was at sea and then a prisoner in South Africa. She asked each of us: "Do you know them?" We both answered: "Yes, it's Mamma and Papa." And she said: "They're alive. They've found you." We were happy and excited—overjoyed.

As we were later told, Mamma had been transferred from Birkenau in late November of 1944, along with three hundred other women, and sent to work at Lippstadt, a subcamp of Buchenwald, in Germany. In early 1945 she was moved again, this time to Buchenwald.

Aunt Gisella, on the other hand, remained in Auschwitz until early January. When it became clear that it was only a matter of weeks until the arrival of the Red Army, the Germans began to dismantle the camp and destroy the evidence of their crimes against humanity. *Kanada*, the crematorium ovens, the clinical records: they tried to get rid of everything. The prisoners were sent on foot to other camps, on the "death marches" that had the purpose not only of transferring the prisoners but of killing them in the ordeal. Aunt Gisella left Birkenau on January 17. She managed to survive that trial, too, and after she was liberated she was taken by the Russians to

Ravensbrück, where she underwent many other brutal experiences. She had to go through what she called a "liberation within the liberation" before she managed to return to Italy. She reached Naples on November 30, 1945, and found her husband, Eduardo, who had returned from prison in Germany. Together, they immediately started looking for little Sergio, while our parents looked for us.

As we later reconstructed it, the first contact between Lingfield House and our family took place as early as May 1946, a few weeks after we arrived in England. But it was some months before the bureaucratic matters were resolved. It seems absurd, but since we were refugees who had been formally handed over to Lingfield House by the British Red Cross, the administrators had to be sure that our family was able to guarantee a decent future for us. An intense correspondence began between Lingfield House and Italy, letters in which the state of our health was described, our story, our emotions. The news that we had been found by Mamma and Papa was conveyed to us a little later, after it was verified that they were indeed our parents and, perhaps, when it was decided that, in fact, we could return to Italy to build a future for ourselves.

Besides, the reunion wasn't something that could happen simply and immediately. This was Europe in 1946, after the war. Documents had to be prepared, a journey arranged that was very expensive at the time. Still, after the summons to Alice's office, it was clear to us that we would leave Lingfield to return home. We wrote many letters to Mamma, in English, obviously, because we had forgotten Italian. At the end of every letter, Andra made a drawing. We still have photocopies of Mamma's answers, which, along with Alice's letters to our parents, are in the Holocaust Memorial Museum in Washington, along with other material regarding the experience of Lingfield House; unfortunately, Mamma didn't save our letters. For a while we were sure she had them. She kept them in her night table. Maybe they were lost during one of the various moves, or maybe, again, she wanted only to forget all the suffering that she, and we, had endured.

In the weeks that passed between our "being found" and our departure for Italy we were really euphoric. We became the center of attention of all Lingfield House, because the hope of finding one's parents was, in essence, the hope of all the children there.

Meanwhile, the Lingfield staff got us ready to leave, giving each of us clothes, a hat, a small purse, a new doll. Some of these objects can be seen in the photo that shows us at Victoria Station in London before boarding the train, published by the *Empire News* on December 8, 1946, with the headline "Sisters for Rome and Home." We're dressed identically, and here, too, we look like twins. That was something that stayed with us for a long time: even in Trieste, as soon as we arrived, people took us for twins. It was also because Mamma continued to dress us the same, which, to tell the truth, was hugely annoying to us!

On December 4 we traveled from Lingfield to London, where we were guests of a cousin of Manna Friedmann's. Saying good-bye to our companions in misfortune we felt a mixture of happiness and sympathy. Miriam, Tati's best friend, was very sad, as she confessed years later when we met again.

We spent one night in London; the next morning, December 5, 1946, along with the social worker assigned to accompany us, we left for Dover and from there crossed the Channel. At the time there was no Eurotunnel, and, as one can imagine, it wasn't easy to travel by air. So we made our journey of return to Italy by train. And what a train! It seemed like the Orient Express, with a sleeping car and a dining car—so comfortable. At some stations, when the train stopped we would get off and jump rope. Just to have some fun. During the trip we were happy and excited that we would at last be able to see our mother. We couldn't wait.

Everything was perfect, until we arrived in Rome. This was our destination because the central offices that took care of reunions and finding missing people and war refugees were situated there. The train stopped at the Tiburtina station. We got out and at the end of the platform, at the head of the train, there was Mamma, waiting for us, standing in front of a car. Around her was an enormous crowd, or at least so it seemed to us. Imagine the scene: two little girls, used to living in the orderly world of Lingfield House, find themselves facing a clamorous throng of people calling to them and questioning them in a language they don't understand.

The news of our arrival, we learned later, had spread through the Jewish community of Rome. Now, it should be understood that at the time, December of 1946, ordinary people had no idea what deportation was. Nor was it clear what Auschwitz had been. Rather, the accounts of the few survivors weren't believed. Society as a whole wasn't ready to take in the words and stories of those who had escaped the horror. What was known was that people had been taken away, but very few imagined the extent of the tragedy or believed in the reality of the Holocaust.

That's why, in that winter of 1946, an entire community saw, in our arrival in Rome, a sign of hope, or at least the possibility of having news of their own loved ones who had been deported between October 1943 and June 1944. There were more than two thousand people about whom nothing was known. Of the twelve hundred who were taken away on October 16, 1943, only sixteen returned. Hundreds of children were deported and murdered by the Nazis in Birkenau. But at the time, their fate was still unknown, and, anyway, a parent's hope never dies. The return of two children encouraged expectations and illusions. All those people were present not only to welcome our arrival but, above all, to get news of their own families, to find out from us if we had seen or met them. They had so many pictures of children and wouldn't stop showing them to us. In addition, they were speaking in a language, Italian, that we no longer understood.

So, bewildered and confused, we walked toward Mamma. Our social worker led us up to her, said good-bye, and left. It was a terrible moment. Overwhelmed by emotions, deserted by the only friend we had, we again felt alone and abandoned, even though our adored mamma was right there in front of us. What a sad paradox! We burst into tears. Mamma didn't know what to do to calm us. She hugged us, kissed us, tried to be loving. We can only imagine the world of emotions she must have felt at that moment. To this day, Andra feels a sense of guilt about that singular meeting, about not having immediately displayed all the joy she felt at seeing Mamma again. But the truth is that we were children who had already been forced by life to confront cruel trials. Tati is convinced that if it had been just Mamma waiting for us, things would have gone differently. But the presence of that crowd, whose very human and at the same time tragic motivations we understand perfectly today, left a distinct mark on our first meeting.

Mamma was alone, because Papa, who had returned from prison in South Africa, had stayed in Trieste and gone back to work. She never told us what she thought or felt as she waited for our arrival. At the station, we got into the waiting car, and went to the house of Giuditta Di Veroli, who had been in the same barrack as Mamma at Birkenau, and who had also survived.

Giuditta and her sister Silvia had arrived in Auschwitz on April 5, 1944, almost at the same time as we did, and with Mamma they formed one of those friendships that could arise only there. They were very close, until the end of their days. And it's precisely as a result of what Giuditta recounted in her testimony that our story began to be known, and that we, too, began to talk about our experience.

At the time, Giuditta lived in the Jewish neighborhood of Rome, at the Portico d'Ottavia, and there, too, in her kitchen, people were constantly coming and going. Mamma very patiently explained to us in German what all those people wanted and tried to be an intermediary between us and them. But we really couldn't say anything to anyone, because in our barrack at Birkenau there weren't any other Italians. We merely nodded, partly because we were afraid of upsetting people by answering that we knew nothing. So most of the time we were silent or spoke Czech with each other.

After several days we left for Naples, to see Aunt Gisella, who had returned to the apartment where she lived before the war, in Via Morghen 65. Today, at that same address, there is a plaque on the door in memory of our cousin Sergio. We were glad to see our aunt, and, after those first hours of disorientation, we had also recovered our feeling of happiness at having found our mother. We returned, finally, to being a family, the two of us and Mamma, and we were just waiting to hug Papa.

Expecting us in Naples were Uncle Eduardo and our cousin Mario, who was just a few months old. He was so little, we affectionately called him Mariolino. We stayed with them for several days. With our aunt, too, we spoke German. She was very kind toward us, then and later. We don't remember what she asked us about Sergio in that first meeting. In fact, after the war, hardly anyone asked us about our cousin. Every so often we talked about him with each other. But in our memory as children, we were immediately convinced that he was dead. Otherwise, we said to each other, he, too, would have returned.

We stayed in Naples for a few days, until Mamma told us that the next day we would leave for Trieste, to join our father. We traveled in a third-class car, with wooden seats. It was an endless, extremely uncomfortable journey. A man sitting beside us was kind enough to lend us a cushion. During the journey all we did was ask Mamma about Papa: how he was, what he thought of us, if he had stayed the same as in their wedding photo. We hadn't seen him since 1940: Tati was only three at the time and had a very dim memory of him; Andra, who was born a few months before his capture in South Africa, had never known him at all. We had waited a long time to hug him again.

STARTING OVER

We don't know how the meeting went between Mamma and Papa after the end of the war, because we didn't speak much about that in the family, either. She returned from Germany, he from prison at the end of 1945: our impression is that they met in Fiume, in the old house where we lived before the war and deportation, and decided together to move from there to Trieste.

In fact, after the war, Fiume, the city where we were born, and where we grew up until our arrest, in 1944, was no longer Italian. Liberated and then occupied by Tito's army, it became part of the Republic of Yugoslavia as a result of the 1947 Paris peace treaties. Mamma and Papa decided to leave the city where they had met, and where he had been born, because they didn't want to live under Tito's communism. They chose to move to Trieste, where Papa could easily return to work; where there was the sea, which everyone liked; and where a less uncertain fate awaited us. Although Trieste, too, was situated on the border between the two countries, and was claimed both by the Italians and by Tito, it hadn't been annexed to Yugoslavia as Fiume had. The 1947 peace treaties established the Free Territory of Trieste, divided into two zones, one administered by the Allies and the other by Yugoslavia, but with the London Memorandum of 1954 the city became fully Italian again.

In early 1946, Mamma had spent a long period in Naples with Aunt Gisella, who, having returned from the camp and rejoined her husband, was again pregnant. She was expecting our cousin Mariolino. Thus it was in Naples that the hope of finding us materialized, thanks to Giuseppe Parlato, a neighbor of Aunt Gisella's, who was the president of the local Red Cross chapter. He helped our mother and our aunt, eventually putting them in touch with Lingfield House.

Arriving from Naples at the station in Trieste we looked out the window and finally saw our father. It was a sight that provoked a powerful emotion, in both of us. Recalling that moment now, Tati is as overwhelmed as she was then. At last we "discovered" our papa. And he was such a kindhearted and jolly person, so good-humored, that from that very moment we were able to cherish and love him. He loved us very much, all three of us.

We spent a few days in Trieste, and then, in January 1947, we went with Mamma to Fiume to fill out the documents of expatriation, that is, the declaration that we chose to remain Italian and abandon Yugoslavia. We stayed there for about a month, the time needed to deal with the bureaucracy and pick up the last things we had. Aunt Tonci was there, along with Papa's brother and Nonna Maria. To this day we can remember our grandmother's indifference when she saw us arrive. We never heard a word of affection from her toward us, not even on that occasion. Our aunt, on the other hand, was very affectionate, as always. She was younger than Papa and loved us. We stayed at our aunt's house, and, to make it more welcoming, she had left the Christmas tree up. We remained very close to her, our cousins, and Uncle Enrico, her husband, in the years that followed. We spent a lot of time together in Trieste, where they, too, moved right after we did. It was an enduring bond; when, for example, in the eighties, our mother became ill and neither of us was living in Trieste, one of our cousins helped us out.

Our relations with our aunt and cousins waned only after the death of our parents. The last time we spent a day together was when we gave our testimony at the Wagner museum in Trieste; even Aunt Tonci came, with her daughter and her daughter's husband. She kept saying to everyone, extremely proud: "Those are my nieces, my nieces!" After that we rarely saw her. But that's also the way life evolves, often leading you, maybe involuntarily, to lose contact even with people you love.

During the month we spent in Fiume Mamma's friends came to see us. They always asked us to repeat the shows we'd put on at Lingfield, and we enjoyed singing and dancing for them. They were all friends of our mother from before the war, and almost none were from the Jewish community. The only former internees we saw were Laura Austerlitz and Marta Ascoli, who had been deported to Birkenau from Trieste.

In late January of 1947, with the paperwork com-
pleted, we took the very few things we could carry from
among those which our grandmother had stored in a
warehouse, and were escorted in a truck by a soldier from
the Yugoslav Army to the border with Trieste. That was
the procedure: at that point we had become foreigners. It
was raining hard that day. Another move, a new exodus
with few explanations, only the essentials that our mother
must have given to two girls. But to us, basically, it seemed
normal. We were used to an itinerant life. And now we
were sure of staying with our parents, and that was enough
for us. Our family was our home. The two of us, Mamma
and Papa. That was partly why we didn't experience the
move from Fiume to Trieste as a trauma; for us it was an
ordinary event. Above all we were too young to realize
that we were leaving the home and the city where we
were born.

Ours is not only the story of two generations that
crossed three empires (the Russia of the tsars, the Austro-
Hungarian Empire, and the Italian) and suffered
persecutions and the Nazi extermination. We also inter-
sected with the exodus of Italians from the zones of Istria
and Dalmatia after the Second World War. We were

among the first to leave those territories. In fact, apart from Fiume and Pola, which immediately became Yugoslavian, the diplomatic negotiations were still going on regarding the rest of the territory, and thus many people were waiting to see how things would turn out. The great exodus took place in 1954, and by then we were permanently settled in Trieste.

After 1947 we rarely returned to Fiume: except in the summer when we wanted to go swimming. *"Andemo oltre,"* "we're going across," people said to their friends, meaning across the border. To go "to Yugo" you didn't use a passport but a card that was called *propusnica*, a kind of permit. We went across the border to get gas, to buy meat and do other shopping, because it was cheaper. Mamma loved Trieste, even though she remained attached to Fiume, her city: where she had grown up and lived with her mother and siblings, who were now dead; where she had been married and her children born.

In Trieste Papa started working for the Allied military government. He became the cook for the harbor commander, a very nice Englishman named Redman, who was fairly old and had a teenage son. Our parents had a Christmas tree to welcome us home, which was a gift from him. At first Papa would have liked to move the whole family to South Africa, but Mamma was against it. Similarly, later, she opposed his idea of having us go to the English school in Trieste: "They're Italian and they should go to Italian school." Mamma made the decisions at home. As they say, it was she who "wore the pants." And then Papa, knowing what she, and we, had been through, tried not to contradict her. He really loved her, and for that reason, too, he was acquiescent. They were very close. We never heard Papa say anything mean to Mamma or vice versa. Only when they got old, then, yes, they had some mild quarrels. But the normal sort. Tati remembers that once Papa slapped her, something that was really rare at the time, and it was because she had talked back rudely to Mamma.

In our first years in Trieste we lived in a very small apartment between the station and the port. After several months, Papa's whole family moved to the city, and Nonna Maria came to live with us, even though Uncle Enrico's apartment in Trieste was bigger than ours: she didn't have a good relationship with him, either.

The apartment had been given to us by Commander Redman. It was in a building divided into two apartments, one for us, the other for an Istrian family. Our part of the house had only two rooms, although they were large: one served as living room and kitchen, with a bed for our grandmother; the other was the bedroom for Mamma, Papa, and us. The bathroom was outside, in the stairwell, with a toilet and a tiny sink. In winter the water was freezing; in spite of that, Mamma made sure we washed carefully every morning. It was very important to her. Once a week we had a bath; the water was heated on the stove and poured into the tub. It was a very small apartment, but we were all together. And that was the important thing. It was near the sea and the English yacht club, where we had permission to go swimming in summer, and when we were little girls the sailors took us around in a motorboat. Even though the water was deep, we learned to swim there. Papa taught us. The naval shipyard was nearby, and so was the Lanterna lighthouse. We lived in that apartment until the summer of 1953.

Living with Nonna Maria was difficult. She called us the *muline*, the bad girls, in dialect. She reprimanded us when we went out with our friends to play in the shipyard—she said we didn't behave properly and were tomboys. To make her happy, Andra would play cards, even though she never liked cards. We don't know if Nonna Maria really didn't love us or if her behavior was simply due to a harsh character. When we were given candies or sweets, we would offer them to her, and, rather than eat them, she put them aside to give to our cousins, Aunt Tonci's children. She'd take them out and offer them to the cousins but not to us. Maybe Nonna still had some prejudice against Jews and had never truly accepted our mother. She stayed with us, in that apartment, until the early fifties, when, to remedy that arduous living situation, she moved to a small apartment in the San Giacomo neighborhood, where every so often we went to see her, prompted mainly by our mother, who would say: "She is your father's mother and so you will go and see her." And we always did it, as long as we lived in Trieste. Nonna died in 1964, right after Tati got married.

Once we were settled in Trieste, we went back to school. Andra was again in first grade, Tati in second. That second half of the school year, from February to June, we went to the Giotto school. Andra was kept back in September because she'd had mumps, and so had frequent absences: she was also kept back because she didn't speak Italian well, even though she did reasonably well in arithmetic and mathematics. If we think about it now, it really seems like one more cruelty after all we had been through. Nor was it random. In the early days, it's true, Italian was a problem: for a long time we continued to speak Czech to each other. It was our secret language; we spoke German with Mamma, English with Papa, Czech with each other. Finally, in school they made us speak Italian only, and asked our family to do the same. Andra felt a great relief in switching to Italian. She said: "Good! So finally we're not speaking those stupid languages anymore." Nonetheless, that couldn't have been the reason that she was kept back in September.

At school, our experiences began to diverge, as they had somewhat at Lingfield. Andra had a very old, conservative teacher who made the girls do crochet, as was the custom then. This teacher tended to reproach and blame her, probably because Andra was Jewish. The old prejudices had returned. It was constant: "Andra, outside!" She punished her for anything. Luckily Mamma understood very well the type of person she was dealing with and took her daughter's side, reassuring and encouraging her.

Tati instead had an exceptional teacher, named Laura Lussi. She asked Tati to tell the whole class her story, the first day of school. Once, and that was all. For Tati it was a relief: the class listened to her in silence. It was as if at that moment her classmates and teacher had understood her need to pull out what she had inside. At school, Tati made a lot of new friends, and Mamma always asked her to take Andra with her when she went out, to help Andra fit in.

In September 1947, with the new school year, we went from the Giotto to the De Amicis, a new and very beautiful school, with a gym and showers. It was at the top of a hill, and we went there by ourselves, every day, always together, there and back; on the way home we'd go running and tumbling down the slope. No matter what, Mamma wouldn't come get us. We had been used to being independent from the start. Maybe she wanted us to be. And we liked it. We never missed Mamma outside school, nor did we think we were unusual because she didn't come to pick us up. It was normal.

Mamma had taught us to be autonomous and generous. One day, on the way home from school, Andra found five thousand lire on the ground—a significant amount at the time. It was just after the flood in the lower Po Valley, and when we got home she told Mamma that she wanted to donate it to the flood victims. And so she did, leaving it at the RAI broadcasting headquarters in Trieste.

At school, we never talked with our friends about Auschwitz. They knew about it, because Tati had told the story the first day, and that was enough. We didn't talk about Auschwitz to each other, either, only about Lingfield, with great nostalgia and regret. The change from England to Italy was difficult at first, especially for Andra, who at meals missed the food that we had every day at Lingfield. In consolation, at night she always had a *ciuffelatte*: it became a fixed habit, a sort of Linus's blanket. During the day with our friends we'd buy licorice, American gum, candy. These were our main "vices." We were just like all children and adolescents in postwar Italy with little money. Tati loved *tavolette di cotognata*, quince jam bars, which she divided into tiny pieces and shared with her friends.

Papa had a steady job with the Allied government in Trieste until 1949. Then he started going to sea again, again with Lloyd's. He was assigned to a ship that had the same name as the one that sank in 1940, when he had been imprisoned: *Timavo*. The ship had just been built and launched in America, and Papa, with some of his fellow sailors, was sent there to get it and embark. In New York he met his American cousins, who were very hospitable, and didn't want him to return to Italy, asking him to stay and even move the family there. But he was adamant. It was as if he were choosing again to return to our family life, which we had lost with the war and deportation.

Papa was paid by Lloyd's only if he was on the ship. That meant that he was away from home for very long periods, because his salary was our family's only source of income. Of course, there were people who were much worse off than us. Papa worked the routes to Africa and the East, and when he was away he always wrote letters, and, now that we were old enough and knew how to write, we added to Mamma's responses our own thoughts or a drawing. Sometimes, when he made a stop in Naples or Genoa, Mamma went to see him, while we stayed in Trieste with Nonna Maria or, when we were a little older, by ourselves.

In 1953 we had to move. We didn't know where to go and asked the city administration for help. At first,

officials wanted to settle us in the Silos, the former warehouse near the station; a makeshift encampment of
Istrian refugees had sprung up there, and just at that
time its numbers were increasing. Mamma and the two of
us were terrified at the idea of ending up there, not only
because of the living conditions that the refugees were
forced to endure, in improvised tents, but also because it
was the same square where we had been brought in the
trucks from the Rice Mill to be loaded onto trains, so as
not to pass through the Central Station in Trieste.
Mamma began to cry when we went to see it. She
said: "I've already given. I will not come here with my
daughters."

It was Uncle Enrico, Aunt Tonci's husband, who
helped us. He suggested that we barricade ourselves in
our house and then he called some journalists from *Il
Piccolo*: a family of former deportees forced to go to a
refugee camp! Imagine the effect when the article came
out. As a result we were offered a place in a new village
of small prefab houses that the Americans were building
on the hill, below Villa Revoltella. And there our daily
life changed, finally. They were nice, comfortable single-
family houses, with a view of the sea. They all had a

kitchen, bathroom, big bedrooms, living room. At first Mamma was desperate because she didn't want to live so far from the center, but we reassured her.

After elementary school we went to the Giosuè Carducci middle school, on Via Madonna del Mare, near the church of Sant'Antonio. Here things greatly improved for Andra. Even in middle school, none of our classmates ever asked us anything. In general no one ever asked about our past. And we had no great desire to talk about it. When, for example, riding on the bus, we hung onto the handholds and the sleeves of our dresses slipped down, revealing the numbers tattooed on our arms, people would ask if it was our telephone number, and we said yes. What should we have said?

In high school, when we were more grown up, we began instead to talk about it a little more, but only with certain close friends, like Lucio Saetti. Everyone more or less knew that we were "the girls who'd been in the camp." That wasn't in itself unusual, given what had happened during the war and afterward with Yugoslavia. What was unusual, but which others didn't know at the time or didn't know much about, was what type of camp we had been in, and why. The Shoah, the deportation, the persecutions did not become common knowledge until much, much later. In those days, when we went to the beach and our friends saw the numbers tattooed on our arms, we said we had been in Auschwitz. And the conversation ended there.

Gradually, our daily life became normal. We often went to Mass on Sunday because our mother wanted us to. Sometimes we went on the bus, the two of us by ourselves. Sometimes, though, we didn't feel like it and, tired of the service, pretended to go while in reality we met our friends in the city. Once, when we skipped the Sunday morning Mass, we met Papa on the bus. We must have been sixteen or seventeen. He sat near us but didn't say anything. When we got home that evening, he still said nothing, while Mamma punished us for a month. No beach, not even in the afternoon. And no walks in the city.

Mamma was like that: very present and protective. On the one hand she pushed us to be self-sufficient, on the other she paid attention to what we did. Maybe she was afraid of losing us again, maybe she just wanted to bring us up in the best way she could and thus make us stronger and more independent. Once, for example, we were going to a party in Trieste and she told us to be home by ten. Naturally we were really late. We were all dancing, enjoying ourselves. It was summer. Would we simply walk out at nine because we had to be home by ten? We stayed until midnight. Our friend Lucio escorted us home. Mamma was waiting for us at the window, arms folded over her chest. She greeted him politely, thanking him, properly. Then she looked at us and said: "It's late now, let's go to bed. You'll pay for this. . . . We'll talk about it in the morning." Another month of punishment. Maybe she wanted to shield us, maybe she thought we were defenseless against boys' advances. Who knows. Often, when she went to see Papa in Genoa or Naples and we stayed home, we'd organize small parties. Luckily our neighbors never "betrayed" us and never told her anything.

That was our mother: a caring and strict woman. And also generous. When she received the pension of a former deportee, including arrears, she decided to celebrate and we all went out to dinner. It must have been the early eighties. She liked to share good things with the people she loved. She was strong and vigilant. She always was, in Fiume, in Birkenau, and, later, in Trieste. It was that generosity, that desire to live in spite of everything, along with her profound love for us, that saved us during the war and enabled us to be found afterward.

We had a close, loving relationship with Aunt Gisella. She came to visit us often, and every summer she and Mariolino spent several weeks with us. Once, when we were still living at the port, we had a huge scare. Mario disappeared; we looked for him everywhere, in the ship-yard, on the wharf, everywhere. Even the men working nearby began to search; they remembered him because he was an endearing little boy with blond curls. Our aunt was literally desperate. She cried and screamed. Sud-denly, Mario reappeared: on the landing in the house there was a dog bed, and, on all fours, he stuck his head out. He had gotten in it and fallen asleep. To this day thinking about it makes us shudder. At the time we didn't really understand, but now our aunt's desperation is clearer to us: it wasn't "only" that of a parent who can't find her child. In her weeping there was all the fear of reliving the loss of Sergio.

We didn't talk about the past with our aunt, either, about Auschwitz and what had happened to us. Just as we almost never did with our father: we talked to him a lot about Lingfield but not about Birkenau. And, especially, we never did with our mother. She, in fact, never mentioned Poland or Germany. Like many other deportees, she wasn't believed when, returning to Italy, she tried to tell her friends what had happened to her in Birkenau and afterward. Then she stopped completely. We don't even know what our parents talked about with each other. To cite an example: one evening, we must have been sixteen or seventeen, we were all at home watching a documentary about the concentration camps on television. Along with Mamma we burst into tears. Papa got up and turned off the television. No one said a word. We went to bed and none of us spoke about it in the following days.

Mamma testified at the trial at the Rice Mill in 1976, when the commander Josef Oberhauser was convicted in absentia. Her testimony appeared in the *Gazzettino* on March 3, 1976. And yet she didn't say anything at home. We didn't find out about it until years later.

That's why we know very little of what happened to her—almost nothing. Besides a very brief interview for a book on the Jews of Fiume, Mamma only once had an interview with the RAI in which she recounted what she had experienced, but only in part, not everything. Unfortunately the interview was broadcast in a reduced, abridged form, and we were never able to find the full recording.

One of the few episodes we know is the story of the scissors. At Birkenau, she was forced to untangle long braids of plasticized material. One day, with a banal excuse, an SS guard attacked her, ordering her to her knees and making her place the point of the scissors she was using against her chest; then she gave her a push to make her fall forward. Mamma saved herself only because she was quick enough to intuit what the German wanted to do and at the last instant moved the scissors away from her chest. Otherwise she would have been dead.

The only person Mamma truly confided in was her best friend: Henny, a younger woman, whom she met after the war. We affectionately called her aunt. Henny came to our house almost every night. She worked as a secretary at the Polyclinic and to supplement her salary she did some sewing; when she came to see us she asked Mamma to help her with the materials and the clothes. All they did was sew clothes and talk, sew and talk. It's to her that Mamma told her story, what she had suffered at

Birkenau, and what happened to her afterward; but she also made her swear that she wouldn't tell any of it to anyone, especially not to us. It was a promise that Henny kept.

Mamma had saved some objects from her experience as a deportee in a trunk in the attic. It was a large attic, where we often went to play. In the trunk was her dress as a deportee, not the one from Auschwitz, probably one they gave her during the various moves, because it had a big red cross on the back, so that she could be recognized if she tried to escape. But then the trunk disappeared. And, anyway, not even when we opened it did Mamma talk to us about Birkenau. Our letters from Lingfield, however, she kept, as we said, in the night table; we looked at those, we were curious. But we don't know what happened to them, either.

We are convinced that Mamma didn't want to talk about what had happened, and especially not to us, as a way of protecting us. She didn't want us to suffer by revealing what she had had to see or undergo, and maybe it was also a way of trying to forget herself. From her point of view, it was an attempt to push us to look forward and not back.

All this—our past, our mother's choices—influenced our relationship with Judaism, which wasn't simple or linear. We returned to it only in recent years, maybe because with age one reaches a greater serenity toward oneself and one's own experience; and, unlike what many think, we don't believe that this recovery of our family identity is connected to the fact that we have begun to testify about our experience as deportees. It was a long and complex journey. Today we feel truly Jewish, especially strong in our culture and inheritance. When Tatiana is asked if she believes in God, she likes to say that she believes in life above all.

At Auschwitz we were aware of being Jewish, but not so much from a religious point of view as because of our condition of life: the *blockovas* had told us that those in the camp who, like us, were Jewish were destined to leave through the chimney.

At Lingfield we began to perceive that our Judaism was something very different. There the staff had us sing songs, dance, discuss our identity. And, as we said, they even taught us some Hebrew. But when we returned to Trieste we were again cut off from Judaism.

Our mother, in fact, wanted us to grow up as Catholics, not out of religious conviction (unlike Aunt Gisella, who had become devoted to St. Rita) but out of her feeling of protectiveness toward us. It was the same motivation that had led her to have us baptized. She also wanted us to take communion and be christened, before we were ten (this is something we've never said before). Basically we were only children, obeying our parents, including going to Mass, as Mamma wanted. For us it was all very simple and natural: school, religion in class, the subjects we studied, the catechism that taught that Jesus died because of the Jews. We even got angry with Mamma because she hadn't been married in church!

We continued to go to Mass for several years, until something happened that led us to break away. One Sunday the priest decided to send us out of the church with a trivial excuse, only because we had been distracted by greeting a friend who had just entered. We didn't like that gesture, and it probably set off something that was already developing in us.

During the years of our adolescence and youth, Judaism remained present in our family in celebrations of the holidays. Every so often Mamma would tell us that this or that holiday was approaching and describe how Nonna Rosa would celebrate it. At Passover, for example, we ate only matzo. Maybe, for Mamma, celebrating those holidays wasn't a religious decision so much as a way of remembering her mother, who was no longer there.

Papa had a serene old age. He was extremely skilled and made extraordinary desserts. After he retired he went to the city center every morning to buy *Il Piccolo*; then he'd go down to the port and meet his friends. It got late, and coming home he'd say to our mother, "*Go incontrà un scoio*"—I met a rock—"and I had to stop." He died in June, 1985, at the age of seventy-nine.

Mamma got sick that summer, right after Papa died. Fortunately Papa didn't suffer much; he went quickly. Mamma instead had a long decline, two years of suffering, in and out of the hospital. She died on August 22, 1987. Tatiana was with her in Trieste, alternating with Andra, who, living in Padua, was always nearby. In the hospital, shortly before she died, she whispered to Tati her last words: "I've had enough." And after two hours in a coma she died. Tati recalls that she didn't cry but thought: "Finally she's stopped suffering." Because in fact Mamma had had one of those illnesses that wear out your soul before your body.

The decision to bury her in the Jewish cemetery was natural. Not only because at the end of her life she had sort of rejected Christianity and recovered her Judaism but also because, over the years, the two of us had found a relationship with our history and our culture of origin. Today, when we go to see her, we offer a greeting and a prayer also for Papa, who is buried in a different cemetery. We put a stone for each of them on Mamma's grave.

TATIANA'S NEW LIFE

When we grew up, we formed our own families. Today we're women who, in spite of our terrible experience, have been able to love, marry, and have children and wonderful grandchildren.

After technical school I began working first for an uncle who had an import-export business, then at the Salus clinic, and then I was the secretary for a doctor in charge of a department. I had some insignificant youthful flirtations, and then I met Gianfranco. I was twenty, and although we were in the same group of friends, we hadn't crossed paths very often. He started to "go after me," as we said in Trieste. We were engaged for six years, because Gianfranco wanted to be settled before getting married. He went to interpreters' school, but his goal—which he later achieved—was to become an official in Brussels, with the European Community.

Gianfranco came from a Trieste family, the Pertoldis. My father-in-law was a gymnastics teacher; they had lived in Ljubljana for several years when Gianfranco was young. Then they moved to Bergamo, where my father-in-law, although he was a right-wing sympathizer, was notable for helping the families of partisans. Because of that, in the confusion that followed the Liberation, the partisans of that area protected him. After the war, the Pertoldis returned to their city of origin.

We were married in Trieste in 1964. I was twenty-six. The first years of marriage were very happy. Living in Brussels, we traveled a lot in Europe. For a short time I worked at IRI (Istituto per la Ricostruzione Industriale) and then, temporarily, at the European Community, near Gianfranco. I liked working, and I was sorry to stop when my sons were born. Once the boys got a little older, I started doing some substituting at the European Community, especially for friends who were pregnant.

Our first son, Stefano, was born in 1968. Mamma had come to stay, to be with me during the birth of my first child. That also made it special. Lorenzo was born in

1970. With both boys I had a very short labor. In fact, Lorenzo was born at home, as we were leaving to go to the hospital; Stefano still remembers coming into our room and seeing me with his little brother in my arms.

When I became a mother, with my children beside me, I had two thoughts. The first for Papa: I knew he would be happy. The second for Mamma: I thought of how she must have suffered when we rejected her in the camp, when her thin, ugly appearance had frightened us. And then, again, at the station in Rome, during that chaotic arrival. Mamma had a warm relationship both with Gianfranco and with her grandsons, whom she adored, although she didn't see them very often, since we lived in Brussels.

I told Gianfranco about my experience in Birkenau right after we met. I trusted him from the start, and it was natural for me to talk to him. He explained my story to his family; his mother had had many dear Jewish friends, who are buried near Mamma's grave; when I go to the cemetery I bring a stone for them, too. I always got along well with my husband's family. Really very well. I never had problems. Even though they were a tradition-ally right-wing family, they never rejected a Jewish daughter-in-law. In fact I was very close to my mother-in-law, and she was tremendously sensitive to our story.

Gianfranco suffered deeply for what I had been through, and he never had the fortitude to go to Birkenau. But he urged me to go and to testify; when I had doubts whether to take part or not in a *Viaggio della Memoria*, a "memory journey," he always urged me to do it, for myself and for others. But he never could bear to go with me. He died suddenly, on August 22, 2018, the same date as Mamma, beloved by his family, while Andra and I were writing these pages.

I didn't speak to my children about my experience until much later; they never asked me what the number tattooed on my arm was, and I considered them too young to know the truth. They began to understand when, in October of 1978, Andra and I went to London for the episode of *This Is Your Life* about Alice Goldberger and Lingfield House. Then, when they got older, they started asking questions.

Most important in enabling me to talk to my children was a phone call from Luigi Sagi. Luigi, known as Gigi, was born in Fiume in 1925. He was captured with his father in late March 1944, and sent to Auschwitz on the same convoy as us. He, too, passed the selection, and he was interned with the number 179605, so almost together with our cousin Sergio. Gigi was among the first to tell his story and to lead students on *Viaggi della Memoria* to Birkenau. At the time—it must have been the late nineties—we had just begun to testify and tell our story in public. I had read an interview with Gigi in a newspaper and noted that he had a number very close to Sergio's. So I made some phone calls to the Jewish community in Rome to find out if I could get in touch with him. When he called me, I started trembling, and nearly fainted with emotion. Stefano was with me, and I have a clear memory of him giving me a chair so I could sit down. I talked to Gigi for a long time, but he didn't remember Sergio.

At that point I began to tell my children those long-ago facts. In recent years they have both been very, very involved. I preferred that they come with me to Auschwitz-Birkenau separately, because having them together would have been too emotionally intense, too difficult. But both visits were wonderful.

I would like to return to Auschwitz with my grandchildren, now that they're old enough to understand. They've begun to ask questions, and I've felt much freer to talk to them, maybe because of age, maybe because of the understanding accumulated over the years, maybe because of the experience I've had with my sons. I always thought Stefano and Lorenzo were too young to be told what I had experienced, but not my grandchildren. I have no idea why.

There was an episode that led me to reflect on this. One day, some years ago, when Luca, Lorenzo's son, was five or six, he was staying with my husband and me. He had a tantrum—which was quite rare—and kept saying he wanted his mamma, the way all children do. So I said to him: "Look, tomorrow Mamma will be here, you'll have Mamma. When we were little, we didn't have our mamma and we never cried." Silence. He didn't say another word. But the next morning, when we were in the kitchen, the two of us alone, for breakfast, he asked me how and why I hadn't had my mamma. I wouldn't have expected that. And so I tried to find the right words to try to explain to him, obviously in the way appropriate for a child of that age.

In recent years I've gone several times to speak in the schools my grandchildren attend. They organized these meetings themselves, with teachers and classmates.

Speaking to children you love, telling your story to your own children or husband, is always harder than with others. You are always afraid of wounding them or making them suffer. Today, at a distance of so many years, I would like to return to Birkenau with my whole family. Health permitting, we'll do it.

ANDRA'S NEW LIFE

After school I started working as a salesclerk at the Standa department store. There I met my future husband, Arnaldo Pezzoni. He was the same age as me, also born in 1939. He was from Bergamo and had moved to Trieste to be the assistant to a manager at the store. He was my only love. We got engaged in 1962, when I was twenty-three, and we were married almost immediately, in Trieste, in October 1963. The wedding was beautiful, even though Arnaldo's family was opposed to our marriage, and not many of his relatives came. Maybe they would have preferred that their son marry a woman of a different class.

My relationship with my husband's family was complicated at the start. My mother-in-law was an elementary-school teacher and my father-in-law a city customs officer. When we lived in Milan and my husband went to see them in Bergamo, I often didn't go with him but stayed home. They truly accepted me only when they learned that I was pregnant. I never talked to them about my story, but they knew, because Arnaldo had told them. Once, my mother-in-law, referring to my being Jewish, asked me: "But what's different about you?" I answered, ironically: "There's nothing different. It's that we're more intelligent." It was my way of saying that, in spite of everything, in spite of all the persecutions, we're still here. My mother-in-law understood. She was a very perceptive woman.

Arnaldo and I moved almost immediately to Milan, where he had found a better position in a paint factory; my husband was outgoing, open, with a lot of imagination, and ambitious; it was important to him to work his way up. He had clear ideas. Arnaldo didn't want me to work, he always said that his salary would be more than sufficient for everything. I gave up work reluctantly, because I would have liked a job, and later, in fact, I had reason to regret it. At the time, however, it was normal to make a choice like that. I told Arnaldo my story almost immediately, over time adding details as they re-emerged in my memory. I trusted my husband profoundly, and it was he who taught me to open up with people, to push myself to speak, to tell. He said it would do me good to pull out those memories. In this, he was very open and farsighted. He was also very close to my parents; he loved them.

Some years later, as Arnaldo was always looking out for a better position, one that would give the family greater security, we moved first to Saronno and then, in 1967, to Padua, where he got a job in another paint factory. The owner took him under his wing, treating him like a son, maybe because he had only daughters. After this experience my husband decided to set up his own business, and it had started to go very well. Fate intervened and again changed everything, because shortly afterward he got sick and died, a rapid, painful death. He died too young, in 1985: we were both only forty-five, and were very much in love. We'd been on a great journey together, which ended too soon and ended badly.

We had two daughters: Mira Tatiana, born in Bergamo in 1964, and Sonia, born in Padua in 1969. The decision to call the first Mira Tatiana was my husband's.

She was born while we were on vacation, in the mountains; she was a month premature, as was her sister. I had chosen Tatiana as her name (which is what we call her in the family), but Arnaldo insisted that she have the first name Mira, like my mother, whom he felt very close to. At first I was a little hesitant about Mira, I had doubts. Not because of Mamma but out of fear of how my in-laws might react. They would have liked us to call her Teresa, like Arnaldo's mother. But there was no way, my husband was immovable. It was a profound gesture of love. I'm still grateful for it today.

My mother was a very sweet grandmother to my daughters. The severity mixed with gentleness that characterized her attitude toward us disappeared with them: the way it is with all grandmothers, basically. She showed her affection, kissing and cuddling them, more, perhaps, than Tati and I were used to with Mamma and she with us.

Arnaldo died in June, two days after my father. I was in Trieste at Papa's bedside when my husband's doctor called me. He had been in the hospital for several weeks, and the doctor told me that in these hours he had worsened; and added, "How dare you leave your husband alone?" I was dumbstruck: I had left for just a few hours to be with my dying father. But there was always someone who felt he had the right to reproach me. Naturally, I hurried back to Padua. Arnaldo was in a coma. I took his hand and said: "I'm here." It seemed to me that he squeezed it. . . . But I was wrong, because right afterward I couldn't hear him breathing and I realized that he was dead. He died just like that.

After Arnaldo's death the real problems began; then I understood the mistake I'd made by leaving my job, but at the time we couldn't have imagined, neither he nor I, that life would separate us too soon. Alone, with two daughters, I had trouble finding work, and Arnaldo's pension, although it was a fairly high level, was unfortunately not very generous. For my part, I hadn't contributed enough to guarantee myself an even minimal early pension; it had been a foolish decision, but Arnaldo said his pension would be more than enough for us. And no one could have imagined that he would be gone so soon. At that point I went from the comfort assured by my husband to difficulty in getting to the end of the month. I'm not ashamed to say that I worked off the books, doing various odd jobs here and there.

When we were in Padua, Aunt Gisella often came to stay with us. And, on those occasions, she told me the story of her liberation and what she had done after Birkenau. She was always the one who told me about our family's travails, about the journey from Russia to Fiume in the early twentieth century. The only subject she never wanted to mention was Sergio. Never, not even in that period. And obviously I didn't press her: it was my way of respecting her suffering.

I've always talked to my daughters about what happened to me, although not very willingly, as one can imagine. But they asked questions. When Mira Tatiana was very young, she began to ask me about the number tattooed on my arm. I tried to answer as one can with a child, without shocking her and without saying tragic things. She was four or five, around my age at the time we were deported. It was then that I really thought about what Mamma must have felt, about her suffering and her courage in the Rice Mill, at Birkenau, and after the war, until we were found.

The older the children got, the more, obviously, they asked. The same thing happened with Sonia. Every time I gave them some further information, I expanded the account. I can say that in the end I had no trouble being open with my girls, and they were always ready to listen to me. Maybe it was because I used the right words.

I believe that our ordeal can be recounted to a child. It always depends on how it's done. And it depends also on the child. Arnaldo agreed that I should explain everything to them, and that was important to me. A few years ago, when my children were adults, they took part in a *Viaggio della Memoria* with me and some American friends of mine. My grandson Joshua also came, and was very moved by the experience. I was afraid of the impact the visit might have on all of us. And in fact my daughters wept, seeing my emotion, and also thinking of their grandmother, whom they were very attached to, and wondering how she had endured all that.

THE RETURN TO AUSCHWITZ

Like many others, we began to tell our story quite late. Our first interview was with Sarah Moskovitz, the American scholar who wrote a history of Lingfield House, and who got in touch with us in the late seventies. Sarah told us she had reached us somewhat by chance, after seeing the 1978 English television broadcast about Alice Gold-berger; a colleague of hers asked if she had ever heard about the children of Lingfield House, and her research took off from there. After interviewing those who had moved to the United States, Sarah decided to come to Europe to meet those of us who had remained there. She also went to Israel and Australia. Thus her research was extensive and thorough.

We hardly talked to her about Birkenau, however, only about Lingfield. Sarah wanted to know about the children at Goldberger's center, and we obviously focused our story on that, saying little about Auschwitz. We mentioned it just to explain to her how we had reached England after the war. When her book was published, we went to the presentation in Los Angeles, along with others who had been at Lingfield House. There, too, we were asked questions, but on that occasion we didn't say much, either, about "before" or about Birkenau. It was a very brief interview, in a collective context. But it helped to give us courage.

We gave our first real testimony—regarding Fiume, the Rice Mill, Birkenau, the Shoah, and all the rest—in 1995, in Trieste. There we really began to speak about our past and compare our memories: fifty years after our liberation from Auschwitz.

It was Marcello Pezzetti, a historian of the Shoah, who found us, through Giuditta Di Veroli, our mother's barrack mate at Birkenau. One day, Giuditta happened to show him some photos and alluded to our story. In essence, we were and are a rarity: two children who survived Birkenau. It wasn't very easy for him to find us, partly because Mamma had died and one of us lived in Brussels and the other in Padua, and we weren't registered in any local Jewish community. When we finally met Marcello, whom we didn't know at all at the time, we talked for the first time in a single voice, as in this book, comparing our memories and our experience. It was an intense and consequential interview.

On that occasion, we also told the story of Sergio, and all our regret emerged that we had been unable to persuade him not to take that fatal step out of the line. It was as if a story—in fact three stories, ours and Sergio's—that for decades had been buried in the deepest depths of memory had finally come to the surface.

In the same period, we also went back to the Rice Mill for the first time. We were hesitant, fearing the impact it might have, and disoriented because of some changes that over the years had been made to the structure. Andra felt a kind of punch in the stomach when we approached the cell where we had been imprisoned. The cell seemed to us truly tiny. She immediately thought of Nonna Rosa, and what she must have suffered. In the following years we went again to the Rice Mill, along with friends, grandchildren, and Mario, Aunt Gisella's son. But Andra would never enter the cell.

During that first visit to San Sabba our thoughts went immediately to the members of our family who had hidden near Vicenza but had later been captured by the Nazis. They, too, had passed through the Rice Mill, some months later. During their detention, Uncle Aaron had drawn on the walls of the cell a mural with the names of all those who were with him: Carola, Silvio, Mario. . . . We first saw the drawing on that visit to the Rice Mill. Then, by chance, we saw it in a 1979 book about the Jewish community of Fiume, a volume that our mother kept on her bookshelf in Trieste but had never really wanted to look at. It was one of her many ways of trying to forget, of repressing what had happened to us.

That visit led us to reflect. Of the thirteen deportees in our immediate family, four of us had returned at the end of the war: the two of us, Mamma, and Aunt Gisella. Four out of thirteen. A very high percentage, if you think about it, but that cannot soften our grief or our pain. Nor can it diminish the homicidal responsibility of those who planned and organized the extermination of an entire people.

We made our first trip to Auschwitz in April 1996. Although after the visit to the Rice Mill we had come around to the idea of starting to truly confront the past, it still took us some months to make up our minds to go to Poland. Some weeks before, at meetings organized by the Auschwitz Foundation in Brussels, we had met the historian Liliana Picciotto, and we told her that finally we were ready.

Andra was still afraid of going: she recalled the experience of Judith Stern, our companion at Lingfield, who had returned from Ravensbrück devastated, and had taken years to recover. She was worried that the same thing might happen to her—that, left alone without a husband, and with her two daughters having recently moved to California, she wouldn't be able to sustain the shock. Tati, too, was reluctant, afraid she wouldn't be able to bear the effect of Auschwitz and Birkenau; she had no idea what to expect or how she would react.

Returning to Poland was a difficult experience, hard for both of us, its impact marked by powerful and ambivalent emotions. In particular, now mothers and grandmothers ourselves, we understood better what our mother must have felt: her courage, her determination, her love for us. For both of us it was another moment of profound empathy with our mother, similar to what we felt at the birth of our own children.

We flew from Milan; in Krakow there were historians and other witnesses waiting for us. We stayed at the Hotel Globe, near Auschwitz, a hotel without pretentions but close to our true goal: Birkenau. Constructed during the Soviet era, it was next to the railroad, and the trains passing in the night kept us from sleeping. Today it's a rundown structure visible from the windows of the bus that goes from Krakow to Auschwitz. But at the time there wasn't much choice: Krakow was not a tourist destination and there were few organized visits to the concentration camps. For several days Sabatino Finzi, who had been deported from Rome on October 16, 1943, and interned with the number 158556, was part of our group. He had been at Auschwitz for several months and then was transferred to Buchenwald, where he remained until the liberation.

That first trip took place in spring, which was a blessing, because Birkenau is very different in winter. The fine weather helped us overcome the effects of our first return. For many of us survivors of Auschwitz, in fact, the most immediate memory of the camp is of the cold, as if we hadn't been through any season except winter. That first time, instead, we saw flowers, grass, daisies— things that were certainly not there in 1944. It was as if it were not "our" Birkenau. If we had arrived with the snow or, worse, the cold, the impact would certainly have been harsher.

As we entered the camp, no one said anything: our escorts deliberately allowed us to speak, and indicate the things and places we remembered. We immediately recognized, with a shudder, the place where the crematorium was. And we pointed out the location of our barrack, which is no longer there. And then the *Sauna*: that, too, we recognized right away. Naturally, in 1944 there was no protective glass over the floor or photographs at the end of the visitors' route. The room where the tattooing had been done was closed and you couldn't visit it.

We went through the Auschwitz Museum quickly with Gigi Sagi; we felt unable to linger in the rooms, looking at the photographs and the objects displayed: eyeglasses, shoes, and everything else that had been left by the Nazis as they fled. There we really felt ill. Tati went back later, by herself, and stayed longer. It should be said that when we're not together, visiting the camp has a different aspect. The first times we supported one another, as if protecting ourselves from the reality represented by Birkenau. Today, so many years later, we have a greater autonomy.

After that first trip, our names appeared in the final list, read by Giancarlo Giannini, in a documentary film from 1997, entitled *Memory*, which assembles testimony of some survivors of the Auschwitz extermination camp. We went to the premiere of the film, in Milan, with Manna Friedmann, who came from London with Andra specifically to see it. About a year earlier, in June, 1996, we had given testimony at the Auschwitz Foundation in Brussels, which, like the testimony we gave to Steven Spielberg's Shoah Foundation, was recorded by each of us individually. When, in 2003, the book *Meglio non sapere (Better Not to Know)*, by Titti Marrone, came out, which tells the story of our family, including us, many friends who didn't know our past were surprised and amazed. With this book, we wanted to tell our story ourselves, directly and in our own voices. We think it's right and perhaps useful for those who would read it.

Our first visit to Auschwitz with students took place in October 2004, on the occasion of the *Viaggio della Memoria* organized by the city of Rome when Walter Veltroni, the mayor at the time, decided to make these trips a regular event. It was an important moment: for the first time we were there to speak to an audience of young people. Maybe partly because of their presence the experience was less painful than we expected. That doesn't mean we weren't emotional: on the contrary. We are always gripped by emotion: even today, when from the bus we see the guard tower in the distance, Tatiana gets a lump in her throat that remains for the entire visit and disappears only when we leave the camp. Andra, too, has trouble going through the gate and can't wait until the visit is over. When she leaves Birkenau it takes her a little while to regain her serenity.

The visits are always very long, or at least they seem so to us. For the kids, however, maybe they pass quickly, because there are so many things to see, testimonies to listen to. Sometimes, too, there are a lot of groups, and that slows things down even more. On the hundred and fiftieth anniversary of the unification of Italy, in 2011, Nicola Zingaretti, as governor of the province of Rome, arranged a trip with seven or eight hundred people. In more than ten years we've met thousands of students, for all of whom the encounter has been truly engaging. One special experience, which we love because it keeps us in close contact with the boys and girls, is the *Memoria* train from Italy to Birkenau organized by the Region of Tuscany.

We believe that the *Viaggi della Memoria* are important because they connect with a delicate subject, with the responsibility that both institutions and individuals should have in making memory something alive. From that point of view, these trips are exceptional, deeply affecting those who take part in them, but they require an extraordinary financial and organizational commitment. To make them succeed, especially with a large number of students, you really have to believe in them.

Over the years we've met many, many young people. The kids have obviously changed and the technologies have changed, thanks to cell phones and so forth. But their gaze, when they visit the camp or listen to our story, is always the same. It is precisely the work that, in the overwhelming majority of cases, the students do on our testimony that confirms how valuable it is to speak in the schools. Maybe the way of working changes, the technologies they use change, but the incentive and the commitment are the same. This is a good sign, a small seed that takes root.

We've never had problems with the students during these encounters, either on the trips to Birkenau or in the schools, or with the adults in the initiatives we've taken part in. On the contrary, we often feel comforted. Once, Tatiana was speaking in Paris, and at the end of the event a woman came up to her and said: "I will never again say that there were no children in Birkenau." Because that, too, was the subject of a heated historiographical debate. We are the living proof of the falsity of the statement.

The most frequently repeated questions have to do with our relationship with our mother, with death, with

God. Our experience is singular, and hard to explain: a strong Jewish cultural tradition that is married to Italian Catholic culture; a journey that has been fostered by a strongly secular approach to life. It's not easy to explain to very young people the sense of God that children of six and four interned at Birkenau could have. We have to help them identify with the little girls we were then, because what they see today is two adult women, grandmothers. And it's also hard to explain that one can feel deeply Jewish even as a non-practicing Jew, or as an "atheist Jew," as Tati calls herself.

Often they ask us (and we have also asked ourselves) why we survived. Why we survived the selection, or why we weren't taken away like other children in our barrack: turning points where our fate might have ended. We don't know the answer. Maybe it was simply chance. We are increasingly convinced that it may also have been our mother's determination, the choices she made, the courage she demonstrated, the strength she indirectly transmitted. While we were in the camp, we weren't afraid of dying. Obviously today we are better able to understand what the situation was. But at the time the thought of death, even so close, never assailed us, or at least not at a conscious level and not in our memories as children. This, too, is an aspect we always have to explain to the students: the border between the reality of Birkenau and the way in which two small children had "normalized" that world in order to survive emotionally.

The students also ask us about our connection with Israel. We were there only once, in the late eighties, on an organized tour. We were in touch with a group of American survivors whom we had met in Los Angeles and we went on various trips with them. The one to Israel was a mixture of pleasure and study, with workshops, meetings, visits to cultural centers and museums. It was a gratifying experience. We were even able to go to the Golan, where we experienced magnificent moments of serenity, and inner serenity as well; we crossed the Jordan River and came to the Dead Sea. In Jerusalem we stopped at the Wailing Wall, even though we aren't practicing, and, obviously, visited Yad Vashem, the Holocaust museum.

We were truly amazed to see a country that had been built out of the desert, to which people had managed to bring water and life. In general, however, apart from the pleasure of that visit, we don't feel a strong attachment to Israel. Tatiana doesn't feel it as a second homeland; Andra, on the other hand, feels a slightly stronger bond, maybe because it was Nonna Rosa's dream, maybe because she feels a close connection with her Jewish heredity and culture. She would never go and live in Israel (although she doesn't deny that, as an adolescent, the idea occurred to her), but she has a dream: to return for her eightieth birthday to run the half marathon there. She is in fact a marathoner, and she trains every day; she started running several years ago, with her younger daughter in California. For the past few years, Andra has divided her time between Italy, Belgium, and the United States to be with her daughters and her grandson. And, in between, she takes part in other initiatives of the *Viaggi della Memoria* wherever she is invited to go.

We find the students from German schools especially affecting; often they don't have the courage to look us in the eye. There is always a high level of participation and they feel directly involved in our stories. Once, a girl was so emotional she couldn't even speak. It's as if they felt guilty for what happened. We try to reassure them, to explain that we know that the German people can't be reduced to what happened to us at Birkenau, and even less those who are so young.

Of course, we have to admit that it took us some time to be able to find a "compromise" with Germany. The encounter with Günther Schwarberg and his wife, Barbara, was crucial in reconciling us with the German people. Tatiana, having lived in Brussels since the sixties, has had many German friends and went to Germany with her husband several times, but it's only thanks to Günther, she insists, that she stopped being afraid: before meeting him, she would never say to an unknown German that she was Jewish and had been in a concentration camp. With him we had an intense exchange of letters, which we have saved.

In any case it should be recognized that in Germany very serious attention is paid to the story of Nazism. We have never had direct relations with the German authorities, but it seems to us that in that country the subject of the extermination is confronted without ambiguity, and with a level of awareness that is different from that of other countries, even Italy, both in terms of historical reconstruction—just think of the great museums that have been built—and at the institutional level, by all those who have been part of the government, whether social democrats, conservatives, or liberals. The first time we were in Hamburg to commemorate Sergio, for example, we were welcomed by the city council, which publicly asked for our forgiveness.

Certainly greater attention is paid there than in Italy, where, with a few exceptions, it's concentrated mainly in the week of Holocaust Remembrance Day, and is otherwise left to the conscience and will of individuals. Of course, things have progressed over the years, but we are far from that widespread shared feeling of respect for memory that can be transformed into a constant and effective civic commitment. And it's especially important to recall that it was not the Germans alone who were responsible for the Shoah. It has been very convenient, over the years, to speak only of them. But we were arrested by Germans and Italians, by Nazis and Fascists; the informer or facilitator of our arrest was an Italian; the bureaucrats who collaborated with the mechanism of extermination that was set up in Italy in 1943 were Italians; the racial laws of 1938 were Italian. And we could say the same thing about other European countries, in the West and the East, where the Nazis were helped by collaborationists. For this reason, too, we should all feel, in a small way, responsible for what happened.

THE REASONS FOR OUR TESTIMONY

We can both say that we had a good life after the war, given the weight of the past that we carried inside us. Most important, we had the capacity to look forward, to imagine the future. Our strength has been our husbands, who understood; our children, who were able to suffer with us and ask the right questions at the right moment; and our beloved grandchildren: Joshua, born in 1994, Luca in 2000, Alessandro in 2002, and Chiara in 2003. In our life we've had many joys and also, like everyone, moments of sorrow and hardship. But a life! Maybe that is one of the most valuable messages we can leave to the boys and girls we meet when we tell our story: demonstrating that, despite the pain and suffering that others may have inflicted on us and those dear to us in the name of an absurd and senseless ideology, we are here. And we didn't only survive: we were able to construct a life for ourselves, a good life. That is extremely important, because it's a message of hope.

The years since we decided to testify about our experience have been crucial, allowing us to recover a piece of our history, to better understand our family and our mother and, at the same time, to be useful to others. We have come to know remarkable people, some of whom are now gone.

We very much admired Shlomo Venezia, who was deported from Greece to Birkenau in March, 1944, like us, and forced to work in the *Sonderkommando*, the group of Jews tasked with removing the corpses of their fellow Jews who had been gassed by the SS. Shlomo began to tell his story later, but, once he started, he didn't stop. He was a very effective narrator and an exceptional person. He traveled with his wife, Marika, who, after his death, inherited his mission. When, during meetings with students, one of us got upset and wanted to cry, he intervened, encouraging her to continue, not to get emotional. For Shlomo, testifying to the very young was a true commitment.

Sami Modiano was also deported from Greece in July 1944, and, like us, he is "Italian by chance." He was born in Rhodes in the brief period when the island was an Italian province. For years, Sami, with his wife, Selma, has participated in the encounters with young people. He considers his testimony a mission, in Italy and on the island of Rhodes, where he still spends the summer, opening the synagogue to anyone who wants to know the history of his community, exterminated by the Nazis.

There is Piero Terracina, who managed to escape the roundup of October 16, 1943, in Rome, but was captured in April 1944, with his family, informed on by an Italian, and transferred to Birkenau. With him, too, we spent very intense moments, hearing the story of his odyssey.

And all the other friends, men and women, too many to mention here, but to whom our thoughts go, along with our affection, and gratitude. To be with them, to share our story, made us stronger, because it allowed us to move from individual memories to the active testimony of history, of what has been. Our lives have become part of a journey, of a common path that has marked us all. Obviously it has marked in different ways those of us who were in Birkenau and those who weren't, those who were born then and those born after the war. In that sense, we are today witnesses of our own lives, but also of the lives of Shlomo, Sami, Piero, and all the others: of the many drowned and the few saved, to use the words of Primo Levi.

Our relationship with Auschwitz hasn't been simple. Andra, for example, feels it very deeply; of course, she doesn't think about it all the time, otherwise she would go mad. But the memory is a persistent presence for her. Tati, with a taste for paradox, upends a comment by the writer Elisa Springer that is often cited during commemorations of Holocaust Remembrance Day ("So great is the risk of forgetting that every day should be an anniversary of Auschwitz"), saying that she feels free to say, "Not every day is January 27" (that is, Holocaust Remembrance Day), or life would be unbearable. If we could construct an existence for ourselves, imagine a future, have a family, it's not only because we were very young when we entered the *Kinderblock*. It's because we did not give in to the sadness of those thoughts but reacted and tried to look ahead: with hope.

Besides, this was one of our mother's first lessons, as she deliberately chose not to harass us with memories. Not speaking about what had happened was, as we've tried to explain, a further means of protecting us. One of the possible means, maybe not the only one, but the one she chose. It allowed us to look forward rather than back. Also, for that reason, unlike other witnesses, we never felt the need to say that "we never left Birkenau." No, we left. In our own way, with our heritage and our difficulties, but we did it, and were able to return. If, instead, our mother had talked to us constantly about what happened, we would have had, we're sure, a different, much harsher life.

It hurts us to see in the world today the return of right-wing, even pro-Nazi parties and movements on the right; to see swastikas on city walls, on flags flying in parades. For people with a history like ours it's unacceptable. It's astonishing to observe what a slender thread memory is, always in danger of snapping. The slightest thing, and no one remembers what happened anymore. Andra maintains that it may also be because of the difficult times we live in, the material deprivations that an increasing number of people suffer. But, she adds, that isn't enough to explain certain regressions. The attitudes of politicians and government officials are also influential: those who tell you that "the one who is different"—yesterday the Jew, today the black person or the immigrant—will take away your job, put social peace at risk and, with it, the tranquility of you and your loved ones. They are "agents of fear" who set off certain impulses in people. That's how it was in the thirties and how it is again today, naturally in very different conditions and contexts.

This return of the ghosts of the past, which is expressed in many ways, from the drawing of the swastika to racism and the fear of immigrants, makes us feel even more responsible. It seems a paradox, right? That we, the victims, feel more responsible. But we do: like everyone else, besides. In the face of what we are seeing, we, more than others, have a duty to recount what happened. Because we were in a concentration camp, because later we were exiles and, although we were lucky in the end, know how exiles are treated: crowded into refugee camps, accused of taking away your job or your home. It happened to the Istrians after the war; it happens today to those who cross the Mediterranean fleeing hunger or war.

Seeing the injustices that are perpetrated around us, seeing people insulted only because of the color of their skin, witnessing a renewal of hatreds and religious persecutions makes us really ill and drives us to tell and tell again, more and more. Today, in our cities, there are still children who die of cold. Today, in our cities, there are still Gypsies, who are considered different and are rejected. There are men and women who are escaping war, hunger, and poverty, hoping for a better future, and whom we treat as criminals, making specious distinctions between war and hunger. As if it made a difference which one you were escaping.

We never speak of these people as people, we don't think of how difficult it is for them to leave their homes, relatives, customs. Italians have forgotten about when they, too, were exiles or immigrants, and how they were treated in Belgium, France, Switzerland, Germany, and overseas. Tatiana remembers, for example, that in Marcinelle, in Belgium, where she lives, there were signs saying "No Italians allowed," exactly as, years earlier, the Nazi signs said "No Jews allowed." It's something that should make us all reflect. The sleep of reason generates monsters: we can't lower our guard, not even for a moment.

People often ask us what Auschwitz has to do with all this, if the memory of what was can help us behave better. We believe that it should, even if, judging from the facts, we sometimes feel discouraged. But then, looking into the eyes of the young people who are listening to us, we find that hope returns, immediately. Speaking about our experience, testifying about it, is crucial for us, because we hope it will be useful to the young. Our conviction is that, if even one of those students has really understood, it will be right to have given our testimony.

Finally, we would like to recount one last episode. Several years ago, in 2015, we were at Mocak, the modern-art museum in Krakow, to see a show entitled "Poland-Israel-Germany: The Experience of Auschwitz," which displayed some of the more controversial and provocative recent works on the Shoah. We were walking through the rooms when, suddenly, our attention was attracted by some music with a compelling rhythm. It came from a video in which young people could be seen dancing at the entrance to Auschwitz. Our first reaction was astonishment mixed with indignation. It seemed to us that they were profaning an image of suffering and sorrow. Then, as we approached, we noticed that in the video a fairly old man, in a T-shirt with *Survivor* written on it, is swaying and dancing with the kids. The video was the work of Jane Korman, who in 2008 had taken her father, Adolek Kohn, a survivor of Auschwitz, and her own three children to Birkenau and other places that were symbols of the Shoah in Europe and had filmed them dancing to Gloria Gaynor's "I Will Survive." Korman, with a mixture of paradox and provocation, was promoting a great message of hope. At the end of the video, her father says, "If someone had told me that sixty-three years later I would return here with my grandchildren, I would never have believed them."

That video made such an impression on us that we said to each other: "We have to come back and do this, too, with our grandchildren."

AFTERWORD: A JOURNEY INTO THE PAST CENTURY

THIS BOOK BY Tatiana and Andra Bucci contains a unique testimony, a story that is at once individual and collective. It's a record of the past that interrogates us, makes us think, forces us to relate to events and times that are at risk of being buried or forgotten. Memory is a powerful tool, and it is what allows the authors to return to that past, with their distinct memories and with their ability to confront and compare situations and moments, recall faces and photographs, retrieve newspaper cuttings or postcards kept for many years in safe places. Their words convey pride in the ability to take hold of the stages of a life, put them in order, seek a meaning.

The sisters' voices come to us from Fiume, a pluralistic city that faces the sea and its distant shores. Italian in a melting pot of identities and cultures, the sisters are used to others, to the many differences—of language, customs, religion—in Europe in the first half of the twentieth century. Journeys and stories meet in a defined space: Italian-speaking populations in the Hapsburg lands of Dalmatia, Istria, and Venezia Giulia; the Jewish diaspora from Central and Eastern Europe, families fleeing ancient discriminations or seeking a better future; the successive stratifications of society as it continuously evolves under the pressure of the industrial revolution, of more or less forced migrations and the processes of nationalization. Points of view and perspectives change as we follow the great transformation of the first half of the century. The world wars are a terrible result.

Overnight, the lives of two children can be turned upside down; like Jews everywhere on the continent, Tatiana and Andra end up in Auschwitz. In April of 1944, barely more than a year from the end of the conflict and nine months from the liberation of the camp, they are catapulted, defenseless and ignorant, into the most atrocious gears of the Nazi extermination machine. From childhood to the camp in Birkenau; from a world open to culture, different identities, and continuous contacts to the closed and cruel reality of the concentration camp universe. But to the eyes of a child even the greatest, most violent tragedy can become ordinary normality, through immersion in a context where horror and death are the order of the day, part of the landscape. How to accept such a burden? What resources can a child's mind muster to remain attached to life and its infinite possibilities of redemption?

It may seem paradoxical or contradictory, but the story of the Bucci sisters contains a message of hope, of love for life and its opportunities. Even at the darkest point, where everything seems to vanish into nothing or into senseless behaviors and practices, one can start again, set off with purpose toward unknown horizons. And so, coming out of the inferno of Birkenau, and passing through the cold, indifferent gray of an orphanage in Prague, Tatiana and Andra are sent to England: to a safe foothold, from which they can return to a full and conscious existence. They are vaulted into happiness: toys, affection, relationships in a community that, under the guidance of Anna Freud, is dedicated to the reconstruction of prospects and hopes for those who survived, often alone. The memories of this marvelous time are precious: Lingfield, in Surrey, is a phase of life that deeply marked the identity of the authors. They could finally turn the page, look for a way out. Their voices fill with nostalgia when they think back to their days in England, to the climate of fraternity and empathy that drew them into a new world.

Their testimony struggles to find words in the continuous balancing act between difficult questions (why did we make it? why us?) and the suffering that, with the passage of time, has become knowledge and memory (many, very many, survivors were unable to reconstruct a life for themselves). It's the unforgiving confrontation between the drowned and the saved that Primo Levi wrote about decades ago, highlighting one of the exposed nerves of the long postwar period we have behind us.

That two children are saved, after being transported to the most horrific death factory conceived and constructed by man, is an extraordinary and in many ways surprising fact. Although the numbers are not certain and are constantly updated, they are pitiless. Some

230,000 children from all over Europe passed through Auschwitz, and only about fifty survived the selections and the Nazi violence, including the insane experiments of the Nazi doctors.

Among those who disappeared into the abyss of the Second World War was the Bucci sisters' cousin Sergio De Simone, born in Naples on November 29, 1937, and deported from Fiume with Tatiana and Andra. He was at Auschwitz with them for several months before taking a path of no return that ultimately brought him to the outskirts of Hamburg. Cruelly tricked by the SS with the promise of seeing his mother, he leaves the children's barrack one morning in November of 1944. He says goodbye to his cousins with a smile, sure they will soon see each other and play together again. This betrayal takes him, along with nineteen other young prison companions, first to the concentration camp of Neuengamme and then to their death in the cellar of a school in Hamburg on April 20, 1945, a few days before Germany's unconditional surrender, when the Allies were at the gates of Berlin. At Neuengamme the bodies of the twenty victims had been devastated by experiments: they had been guinea pigs, to be annihilated among the compromising evidence of crimes against humanity. Tatiana and Andra's cousin was killed with the others, hanged on a hook on the wall of the cellar: "like paintings on the walls," one of the perpetrators of the crime confessed at the trial, in 1946.

Sergio didn't hesitate: at the word "mamma," he stepped forward, to return to the arms of the person who brought him into the world. How many regrets in the hearts of the authors that they failed to prevent that move, to protect their cousin. That one life is worth all lives and is bound into the sisters' testimony: they speak of it as if it were a duty, a message to hand down, a story that has to be defended from the risk of being forgotten or repressed.

Sergio is a constituent part of the testimony in these pages, representing the other extreme, those who didn't make it, and who deserve attention, respect, sympathy. His fate emerges as the legacy of a family tragedy: the killing of an innocent child becomes an integral part of the story in two voices that should have included a third, who did not survive. From the moment it was possible to reconstruct the details of the fate of the children taken away from Birkenau, the story in two voices became broader, trying to give space and representation to those who could no longer speak for themselves.

Tatiana and Andra remained at Auschwitz until the liberation, January 27, 1945, perhaps taken for twins or spared by an unpredictable trick of fate. As they say in an interview, "We were guarded and protected by a *blockova*. We don't remember anything about her, neither her name nor her face, not even her physical features." They lived through the darkest times of our past and have emerged to become tireless witnesses, among the few who can still convey what their eyes saw.

When they go to Auschwitz with Italian young people and students, they stop to speak in front of the children's barrack where they spent almost ten months of their childhood. Only the brick perimeter of the building remains, the vestiges of a structure that one can only imagine or track down among the documents in the archive. As in these pages, when the sisters are in a public setting they take turns speaking, and a single voice seems to bear the weight of their testimony. The sisters accompany school-children and institutions, large or small groups, by airplane, train, or bus, traveling from Italy to Poland, where the Nazi death installations were built. These are educational journeys, an exchange of experiences and languages between generations in search of a connection. Tatiana and Andra don't shrink from this; they indefatigably engage in contemporary forums, and even have a presence on social media, where they trade images and reflections with young people all over the world.

We know how difficult it has been for survivors to find the strength and the words to tell their story, to break their silence in the face of those who were not ready to hear about that terrible past. Even Primo Levi had trouble finding a publisher who was interested and committed; Shlomo Venezia has told of being silenced by the reactions of those who thought he was mad when he began to share fragments of his earlier life. Silence thus became an apparent refuge, waiting for time and individual conviction to mature. The reactions of the survivors are many and diverse: some are closed in on themselves, some have continued to live with recurring nightmares and depression, some followed friends or companions ready to let go of their suffering in words and phrases; some, not encountering an encouraging or sympathetic audience, found themselves alone, burdened by questions and painful memories.

In this picture, the testimony of the Bucci children, who survived Auschwitz, has an extraordinary value: the force of life and the defense of it against any giving in. The era of the witness began more than half a century ago and has perhaps entered its last phase, given the time that separates us from the events and the path that has marked the life of so many who found the strength and the capacity to speak. Any testimony added is therefore precious, a human patrimony to hand down to those who will come after us to read, listen to, and recount to future generations.

Tatiana and Andra Bucci began their journey as witnesses almost by chance, with an interview on the BBC and, after that, in the prestigious setting of the archive of the Fondazione Centro di Documentazione Ebraica di Milano (CDEC). They continued to bear witness, reinforcing the meaning of their testimony. They were girls who returned from an extermination camp, Jews who got out of a sentence that had been written and codified, children who found their mother, and an embrace that unites after the violent separation of the war.

Over time their voice has become familiar to those who organize the Viaggi della Memoria and other educational trips. The sisters travel from Brussels, from Padua, from Sacramento (where their lives have taken them over the years) to contribute, to deliver their testimony to those they meet. After many years of hearing their elegant and precise talks, within the perimeter of the camp, on the ruins of the children's barrack, or just outside of what remains of the Kinderblock, we learned that they wanted to try to leave a more durable testimony: to write a book, a gift that would last over time. Thanks also to the commitment of the Fondazione Museo della Shoah in Rome, it was possible to respond to Tatiana and Andra's wish. We began meeting in a small group to record and investigate sources and documents, starting with the traces of those who had followed, in part, the same route as Tatiana and Andra: Teodoro Morgani and his portrait of the Jews of Fiume (*Ebrei di Fiume e di Abbazia, 1441-1945 [The Jews of Fiume and Abbazia, 1441-1945]*), the chapters devoted to the Bucci sisters in Sarah Moskovitz's book on the work of recovery and reinsertion of children who escaped from the Shoah to postwar England (*Love Despite Hate: Child Survivors of the Holocaust and Their Adult Lives*), and finally Titti Marrone's retelling of the story of Tatiana, Andra, and Sergio (*Meglio non sapere [Better Not to Know]*). But there was a missing tile, and that became the goal of the shared work, a goal that Tatiana and Andra insistently expressed a wish to achieve: a book, a complete testimony that would give them the opportunity to assemble and put in order the various parts of their lives.

That is the origin of this book. It's an attempt to emerge from a false choice between a past that sinks and a present that slides easily into oblivion. The story of Tatiana and Andra is also a story of success and happiness, of mothers and grandmothers who in the decades after the war were able to construct families, hopes, possibilities. They offer a warning against discriminations old and new, surfacing in a dangerous time. Ghosts of the past that seemed conclusively defeated emerge: rising nationalisms, forms of prejudice against the different, more or less masked racism that takes aim at the guilty of the moment, the immigrant or the weakest link in a chain of suffering. Bearing witness is also a way of driving out fears and vanquishing those who create and circulate them as if history had nothing to teach us. *Always Remember Your Name* is a story, a testimony, the confirmation that we can look ahead even when everything seems to go in the opposite direction, when the road appears blocked and with no exit.

It's hard to find words to thank the authors for their generosity, for their humility in immersing themselves in the events of a distant time, for the courage and strength to reopen wounds that have never completely healed. Those who have the patience to read and to tell this story of the past century have a duty not to waste the value of a memory, the meaning of a collective responsibility that can unite us in a common destiny. Without rhetoric: to know in order not to forget, today, tomorrow, and forever.

—UMBERTO GENTILONI SILVERI, ROME, 2018

ACKNOWLEDGMENTS

For the publication of our book in English, we have to thank, first of all, Barbara Pierce. As soon as she read it, she first set out to find a translator and then a publishing house that was willing to publish it. She didn't give up when things got tough, because of the pandemic—she's like a train charging full speed ahead!

Further, we must thank the former Italian consul in San Francisco, who gave our book to his mother-in-law to read, as his mother-in-law is Barbara Pierce.

A special thanks to Andra's daughter Sonia, who helped us with the correspondence and in reviewing the English translation. She was a perfect secretary.

We also thank our "star" that always protected us and brought us home, so that we could tell our story.

And last but not least, thank you to the team at Astra House, who had the courage to take on this adventure.

ABOUT THE AUTHORS

Andra (b. 1939) and Tatiana Bucci (b. 1937) were born in Fiume, the daughters of a Catholic father and Jewish mother. They were deported to Auschwitz along with their mother, grandmother, aunt, and a cousin. When the camp was liberated, in 1945, they were sent first to Czechoslovakia and later to England, where their parents finally tracked them down. They were reunited with their parents in 1946. Today, they bear witness in schools and at the camps.

ABOUT THE TRANSLATOR

Ann Goldstein is a former editor at *The New Yorker*. She has translated works by, among others, Elena Ferrante, Pier Paolo Pasolini, and Alessandro Baricco, and is the editor of the *Complete Works of Primo Levi* in English. She has been the recipient of a Guggenheim fellowship and awards from the Italian Ministry of Foreign Affairs and the American Academy of Arts and Letters.

READING GROUP GUIDE

- Members of the Bucci family were very close, and yet the girls' Catholic grandmother's family in Istria refused to help them. Why do you think that is? What does this tell us about family dynamics in general and about Italian society under Fascism?

- Why did the Buccis stay in Fiume even as their family members and neighbors hid or fled? How did the chaos of the war and their father's incarceration in South Africa affect their understanding of what was happening and influence their choices?

- In the end it was the women and children of the Bucci family who were deported to Auschwitz-Birkenau. How does this put into relief or challenge established gender roles in families at the time? How does Mira's maternal love intersect with her survival instinct? How do the routines she created for the girls before the war help them while they were in Birkenau and afterward? How does the girls' relationship with their mother transform over the course of the memoir? How does it stay the same?

- The photograph of Tati and Andra's parents on their bedside table in Fiume plays a key role in their reunion. The sisters' father is absent for much of the narrative but still looms large. What role does his absence play in the girls' ordeal? How might things have been different had he been home with them during the war?

- The sisters' cousin Sergio comes to a tragic end in spite of their effort to warn him. What do you think moved him to believe the guards' lie? What role does chance play in a life-and-death situation like this?

- This is a very rare testimony of children who survived Auschwitz. In the memoir, the children didn't always seem fully aware of what was happening at the camp, or why they were there, and yet they saw the horrors and suffered tremendously. How do the authors' young ages make this memoir different from other Holocaust memoirs? How did their youth shape the impact the horrors had on them?

- How does the fact that the memoir is in two voices—at times speaking as one, at times in conversation—affect the reading experience? How is the strong bond between the sisters reflected in these pages and how is it reflected in the fact of their survival?

■ In some ways, this account picks up where Anne Frank's diary left off. Very few children survived Auschwitz, but the Bucci sisters were among them. Some of the things that seem most likely to have increased Tati and Andra's chances for survival (having each other, their mother's presence) were also true of Anne, who was in Auschwitz together with her older sister, Margot, and their mother. But Anne was treated as an adult in Auschwitz, required to work, while the younger children weren't. Can you think of other literature about the Holocaust that discusses the arbitrariness of survival in the campo? What possible explanations do Primo Levi, Elie Wiesel, or others give for the miracle of their survival?

It takes a village to get from a manuscript to the printed book in your hands. The team at Astra House would like to thank everyone who helped to publish *Always Remember Your Name.*

PUBLISHER

Ben Schrank

EDITORIAL

Alessandra Bastagli

Olivia Dontsov

CONTRACTS

Stefanie Ratzki

PUBLICITY

Rachael Small

MARKETING

Tiffany Gonzalez

Sarah Christenson Fu

Jordan Snowden

SALES

Jack W. Perry

DESIGN

Jacket: Rodrigo Corral Studio

Interior: Richard Oriolo

Jeanette Tran

PRODUCTION

Lisa Taylor

Alisa Trager

Rebecca Baumann

COPYEDITING

Rachel Broderick

COMPOSITION

Westchester Publishing Services

ABOUT ASTRA HOUSE

Astra House is dedicated to publishing authors across genres and from around the world. We value works that are authentic, ask new questions, present counternarratives and original thinking, challenge our assumptions, and broaden and deepen our understanding of the world. Our mission is to advocate for authors who experience their subject deeply and personally, and who have a strong point of view; writers who represent multifaceted expressions of intellectual thought and personal experience, and who can introduce readers to new perspectives about their everyday lives as well as the lives of others.